ASP.NET MVC IN 7 DAYS

BY

ER. VAIBHAV SINGH CHAUHAN

वक्रतुण्ड महाकाय सूर्यकोटिसमप्रभ।

निर्विघ्नं कुरु मे देव सर्वकार्येषु सर्वदा॥

DEDICATING THIS BOOK TO THE UNIVERSE WITHIN

ABOUT AUTHOR

ER. VAIBHAV SINGH CHAUHAN IS A SOFTWARE CONSULTANT HAVING WIDE EXPERIENCE WORKING IN A CORPORATE ENVIRONMENT. HE HAS SERVED AS PROJECT LEADER AND TEAM LEAD IN SOME REPUTED ORGANIZATIONS WORKING FOR SWEDISH, US, UK, JAPANESE, AND INDIAN CLIENTS. .NET TECHNOLOGY IS THE FOUNDATION TECHNOLOGY THROUGH WHICH HE STARTED HIS CAREER. SO HE HAS A SOUND KNOWLEDGE OF THE PLATFORM AND SERVICES USED.

WEBSITE : https://vaibonline.com

EMAIL : ER_VAIBHAVSINGH@YAHOO.COM

INTRODUCTION

"ASP.NET MVC IN 7 DAYS" IS AN IMMERSIVE GUIDE THAT TAKES YOU THROUGH A COMPREHENSIVE JOURNEY OF LEARNING AND MASTERING ASP.NET MVC, A POWERFUL WEB FRAMEWORK DEVELOPED BY MICROSOFT. THE BOOK IS STRUCTURED INTO SEVEN DAYS, EACH FOCUSING ON KEY ASPECTS OF ASP.NET MVC DEVELOPMENT, GRADUALLY BUILDING YOUR EXPERTISE FROM THE FUNDAMENTALS TO ADVANCED TOPICS.

DAY 1-2: GETTING STARTED

THE JOURNEY BEGINS WITH AN INTRODUCTION TO ASP.NET MVC, GUIDING YOU THROUGH SETTING UP YOUR DEVELOPMENT ENVIRONMENT AND UNDERSTANDING THE MVC DESIGN PATTERN. YOU CREATE YOUR FIRST MVC APPLICATION, EXPLORING THE PROJECT STRUCTURE AND LAYING THE FOUNDATION FOR THE DAYS AHEAD.

DAY 3: BUILDING THE MODEL

THIS DAY FOCUSES ON THE MODEL IN MVC. YOU DIVE DEEP INTO UNDERSTANDING MODELS, CREATING MODEL CLASSES, IMPLEMENTING DATA ACCESS WITH ENTITY FRAMEWORK, AND INCORPORATING DATA ANNOTATIONS FOR VALIDATION. TESTING MODEL CLASSES ENSURES THEIR RELIABILITY.

DAY 4: DEVELOPING THE VIEWS

YOU SHIFT YOUR ATTENTION TO CREATING ENGAGING USER INTERFACES. THIS DAY COVERS THE CREATION OF VIEWS, WORKING WITH RAZOR SYNTAX, IMPLEMENTING LAYOUTS, FORMS, AND HTML HELPERS. STYLING AND

CUSTOMIZATION ARE EXPLORED TO ENHANCE THE VISUAL APPEAL OF YOUR APPLICATIONS.

Day 5: Controllers and Routing

Delving into the core of MVC, you learn about controllers and routing. Implementing controller actions, handling parameters, and mastering routing techniques are central to efficiently managing user requests. Error handling and exception management are also covered.

Day 6: Working with Data and Entity Framework

This day focuses on data operations. You learn to retrieve, display, sort, filter, update, and delete data using Entity Framework. Advanced querying techniques are explored for efficient data manipulation.

Day 7: Advanced Topics and Best Practices

The final day covers advanced topics, emphasizing performance optimization through caching. You work with Web API and JSON serialization, integrate client-side technologies (JavaScript, jQuery), and delve into unit testing and test-driven development (TDD). The book concludes with deployment strategies, hosting options, and security considerations.

Conclusion: Journey Towards Mastery

The book concludes by celebrating your journey to mastery. You've not only learned the technical intricacies of ASP.NET MVC but also acquired best practices for deployment, hosting, and security. The summary encourages continuous learning, exploration of new features, and the application of knowledge to real-world projects.

Key Takeaways:

- Understanding of MVC architecture and its advantages. - Proficient setup of the development environment.

- In-depth knowledge of models, views, and controllers.

- Expertise in Entity Framework for data access.

- Implementation of authentication, authorization, and security measures.

- Integration of client-side technologies for enhanced user experiences.

- Mastery of deployment strategies and hosting options.

"Mastering ASP.NET MVC in 7 Days" serves as a comprehensive guide, equipping readers with the skills needed to develop scalable, secure, and efficient web applications using ASP.NET MVC.

Table of Contents:

4. Implementing Forms and HTML Helpers

5. Styling and Customizing Views

Day 4: Controllers and Routing

1. Introduction to Controllers

2. Implementing Controller Actions

3. Parameter Binding and Model Binding

4. Routing in ASP.NET MVC

5. Handling Errors and Exceptions

Day 5: Working with Data and Entity Framework

1. Retrieving and Displaying Data

2. Sorting and Filtering Data

3. Implementing Paging and Pagination

4. Updating and Deleting Data

5. Implementing Advanced Querying Techniques

Day 6: Authentication and Authorization

1. Introduction to Authentication and Authorization

2. Implementing User Registration and Login

3. Securing Controllers and Actions

4. Implementing Role-Based Authorization

5. Customizing Authentication and Authorization

Day 7: Advanced Topics and Best Practices

1. Implementing Caching for Performance Optimization

2. Working with Web API and JSON Serialization

3. Integrating Client-Side Technologies (JavaScript, jQuery)

4. Unit Testing and Test-Driven Development (TDD)

5. Deployment and Hosting Options

Conclusion: Journey Towards ASP.NET MVC Mastery

Day 1: Getting Started with ASP.NET MVC

Welcome to Day 1 of your journey to mastering ASP.NET MVC! In this chapter, we will introduce you to the fundamental concepts of ASP.NET MVC and provide you with a solid understanding of its benefits and architecture.

Chapter 1: Introduction to ASP.NET MVC

1.1 What is ASP.NET MVC ?

ASP.NET MVC is a web application framework developed by Microsoft that follows the Model-View-Controller (MVC) architectural pattern. It provides a structured approach to building dynamic, scalable, and maintainable web applications. Unlike traditional web forms, ASP.NET MVC separates the concerns of data presentation, data processing, and data storage, resulting in a more modular and testable codebase.

1.2 Key Features and Benefits

ASP.NET MVC offers several key features that make it a popular choice among developers:

a. Separation of Concerns: The MVC pattern promotes a clear separation of concerns, allowing developers to focus on specific aspects of the application independently. Models handle data management, views handle user interface rendering, and controllers handle user interactions and orchestrate the flow of data.

b. Testability: With the separation of concerns, ASP.NET MVC applications are highly testable. You can easily write unit tests for individual components, making it easier to identify and fix issues during development.

c. Extensibility: ASP.NET MVC provides a highly extensible framework, allowing developers to customize and extend its behavior to meet specific project requirements. You can create custom model binders, filters, view engines, and more.

d. URL Routing: Routing is a crucial aspect of ASP.NET MVC. It enables you to define clean, search engine-friendly URLs that map to specific controller actions. Routing makes it easier to implement RESTful web services and creates user-friendly URLs for better user experience.

e. Support for Client-Side Technologies: ASP.NET MVC seamlessly integrates with popular client-side technologies like JavaScript, jQuery, and CSS frameworks. This enables you to build interactive and responsive user interfaces.

1.3 Understanding the MVC Pattern

The Model-View-Controller (MVC) pattern is a software design pattern that separates an application into three interconnected components:

a. Model: The model represents the application's data and business logic. It encapsulates data access, validation rules, and behavior specific to the application's domain. In ASP.NET MVC, models are typically represented by classes.

b. View: The view is responsible for presenting the data to the user. It defines the user interface and controls how data is displayed. Views in ASP.NET MVC are usually created using Razor syntax or other templating engines.

c. Controller: The controller handles user interactions, processes user input, and determines the appropriate response. It receives input from the user through the view and interacts with the model to retrieve and manipulate data. Controllers in ASP.NET MVC are responsible for coordinating the flow of data between the model and the view.

1.4 ASP.NET MVC Architecture

ASP.NET MVC follows a layered architectural approach. The key components of an ASP.NET MVC application are:

a. Models: Models represent the application's data and business logic. They are responsible for data access, validation, and behavior. Models are typically implemented using Plain Old CLR Objects (POCOs) or Entity Framework for database interactions.

b. Views: Views are responsible for rendering the user interface. They receive data from the controller and present it to the user in a specified format, such as HTML. Views can be plain HTML with embedded code or use a templating engine like Razor.

c. Controllers: Controllers handle user interactions, process requests, and orchestrate the flow of data. They receive user input from the view, interact with the model to retrieve and manipulate data, and select the appropriate view to display the results.

d. Routing: Routing maps URLs to specific controller actions. It determines which controller and action should be executed based on the requested URL. Routing allows you to define custom URL patterns and implement clean and search engine-friendly URLs.

1.5 Setting up the Development Environment

Before diving into ASP.NET MVC development, you need to set up your development environment. You will require:

a. Visual Studio: Microsoft Visual Studio is a powerful integrated development environment (IDE) that provides a comprehensive set of tools for building ASP.NET MVC applications. You can download the latest version of Visual Studio from the Microsoft website.

b. .NET Framework: ASP.NET MVC relies on the .NET Framework for its runtime execution. Ensure that you have the appropriate version of the .NET Framework installed on your development machine.

Once you have the necessary tools installed, you are ready to start building your first ASP.NET MVC application!

Exercises:

1. Research and list three popular websites or applications built using ASP.NET MVC.

2. Compare and contrast the MVC architectural pattern with the traditional Web Forms approach.

3. Install Visual Studio and the .NET Framework on your development machine, if you haven't already.

Chapter 2: Setting up the Development Environment

2.1 Installing Visual Studio

Microsoft Visual Studio is the preferred integrated development environment (IDE) for ASP.NET MVC development. It provides a range of tools and features to streamline your development process. Follow these steps to install Visual Studio:

1. Visit the official Visual Studio website (https://visualstudio.microsoft.com) and download the latest version of Visual Studio.

2. Run the installer and follow the on-screen instructions. You can choose the workload that includes ASP.NET and web development tools.

3. Select the desired components and options based on your requirements.

4. Once the installation is complete, launch Visual Studio.

2.2 Installing the .NET Framework

The .NET Framework is the runtime execution environment for ASP.NET MVC applications. Ensure that you have the appropriate version of the .NET Framework installed on your development machine. Here's how you can install it:

1. Visit the Microsoft .NET website (https://dotnet.microsoft.com) and download the latest version of the .NET Framework.

2. Run the installer and follow the instructions provided.

3. Select the desired options and components based on your requirements.

4. Once the installation is complete, verify that the .NET Framework is installed by opening a command prompt and running the following command: `dotnet --version`. It should display the installed version of the .NET Framework.

2.3 Creating a New ASP.NET MVC Project

Now that you have Visual Studio installed and the .NET Framework set up, let's create your first ASP.NET MVC project:

1. Open Visual Studio.

2. Click on "Create a new project" or go to "File" > "New" > "Project".

3. In the project creation window, select "ASP.NET Web Application" from the available project templates.

4. Choose a project name and location.

5. Select "ASP.NET Core" as the project type.

6. Choose the desired project template, such as "Web Application" or "Empty", depending on your needs.

7. Click "Create" to create the project.

8. In the project configuration window, select the desired options for authentication, such as "Individual User Accounts" or "No Authentication".

9. Click "Create" to create the project.

Visual Studio will generate the necessary project structure and files for your ASP.NET MVC application.

2.4 Exploring the Project Structure

Understanding the project structure is essential for working with ASP.NET MVC. Let's explore the basic structure of an ASP.NET MVC project:

1. Solution: A solution is a container for one or more projects. It provides a way to organize and manage related projects together. In Visual Studio, the solution file has the extension `.sln`.

2. Project: A project represents an individual application or component within a solution. In an ASP.NET MVC project, the main project contains the MVC application and its associated files. The project file has the extension `.csproj` for C# projects.

3. wwwroot: The `wwwroot` folder contains static files such as CSS, JavaScript, images, and other assets that are directly served to clients.

4. Controllers: The `Controllers` folder contains the controller classes. Controllers handle user interactions, process requests, and coordinate data flow between models and views.

5. Models: The `Models` folder holds the model classes that represent the application's data and business logic. Models are responsible for data access, validation, and behavior.

6. Views: The `Views` folder contains the view templates responsible for rendering the user interface. Views use the Razor syntax or other templating engines to generate dynamic HTML content.

7. Startup.cs: The `Startup.cs` file contains the configuration for your application, including services, middleware, and routing configuration. It is the entry point for configuring your ASP.NET Core application.

2.5 Running the Application

To run your ASP.NET MVC application and see it in action, follow these steps:

1. Build the project by selecting "Build" > "Build Solution" or pressing `Ctrl + Shift + B`.

2. Once the build process completes successfully, click on the "Play" button or press `F5` to start debugging.

3. Visual Studio will launch a web browser and navigate to the default URL of your application, such as `https://localhost:5001` or `http://localhost:5000`.

Congratulations! You have successfully set up your development environment, created an ASP.NET MVC project, and explored its basic structure.

Exercises:

1. Install Visual Studio and the .NET Framework on your development machine if you haven't done so already.

2. Create a new ASP.NET MVC project using Visual Studio and explore its project structure.

3. Run the application and verify that it is working correctly.

Chapter 3: Understanding the MVC Design Pattern

3.1 Recap: What is the MVC Design Pattern?

The MVC design pattern is a software architectural pattern that separates an application into three interconnected components: the Model, View, and Controller. Let's recap the responsibilities of each component:

a. Model: The Model represents the application's data and business logic. It encapsulates data access, validation rules, and behavior specific to the application's domain. In ASP.NET MVC, models are typically represented by classes.

b. View: The View is responsible for presenting the data to the user. It defines the user interface and controls how data is displayed. Views in ASP.NET MVC are usually created using Razor syntax or other templating engines.

c. Controller: The Controller handles user interactions, processes user input, and determines the appropriate response. It receives input from the user through the View and interacts with the Model to retrieve and manipulate data. Controllers in ASP.NET MVC are responsible for coordinating the flow of data between the Model and the View.

3.2 Benefits of the MVC Design Pattern in ASP.NET MVC

The MVC design pattern offers several benefits when applied to ASP.NET MVC development:

a. Separation of Concerns: By separating the application into distinct components, the MVC pattern promotes a clear separation of concerns. Each component has a specific responsibility, making the codebase more modular and easier to maintain.

b. Testability: The MVC pattern enhances testability as each component can be tested independently. Models can be tested for data access and business logic, Views can be tested for UI rendering and data presentation, and Controllers can be tested for handling user interactions and data flow.

c. Reusability: The separation of concerns allows for greater code reuse. Models, Views, and Controllers can be used across different parts of the application or even in different applications, resulting in more efficient development.

d. Flexibility: ASP.NET MVC's implementation of the MVC pattern provides flexibility and extensibility. You can customize and extend the behavior of each component to meet specific project requirements. For example, you can create custom model binders, filters, view engines, and more.

e. Scalability: The MVC pattern supports the development of scalable applications. As the codebase is organized into separate components, it becomes easier to manage and scale individual parts of the application independently.

3.3 MVC Workflow in ASP.NET MVC

Understanding the flow of data and interactions in the MVC pattern is essential for effective ASP.NET MVC development. Here's a high-level overview of the typical workflow:

1. The user interacts with the application by sending a request, such as clicking a link or submitting a form.

2. The request is first received by the Controller. The Controller determines the appropriate action based on the requested URL and other parameters.

3. The Controller interacts with the Model to retrieve or update data as required. It may call methods in the Model to perform data access, validation, or other business logic operations.

4. Once the necessary data is processed, the Controller selects the appropriate View to render the response. The Controller passes the data to the View, typically in the form of a strongly-typed Model object.

5. The View uses the data passed by the Controller to generate the HTML markup, which is then sent back as the response to the user's request.

6. The user's browser receives the response and displays the rendered View to the user.

7. If the user interacts with the rendered View (e.g., submitting a form or clicking a link), the cycle repeats as a new request is sent to the Controller, and the process starts again.

3.4 Understanding View Templates

In ASP.NET MVC, Views are created using view templates. The most commonly used view template engine is Razor, which allows mixing HTML and server-side code within the same file. Razor views have the `.cshtml` extension.

View templates use Razor syntax to combine HTML markup with server-side code. This enables dynamic generation of HTML content based on data from the Model. Razor provides various constructs such as expressions, conditional statements, loops, and more, to manipulate and render data.

3.5 Layouts and Partial Views

Layouts and Partial Views are essential components of ASP.NET MVC's View system:

a. Layouts: A Layout is a shared template that defines the common structure and elements for multiple Views. It typically includes elements such as header, footer, navigation, and sidebars. Views can specify a Layout to inherit from, allowing consistent UI across multiple pages.

b. Partial Views: Partial Views are reusable components that can be included within other Views or Layouts. They encapsulate a specific section of UI functionality, such as a sidebar, a user profile widget, or a comment section. Partial Views allow for modular and reusable UI components.

3.6 Styling and Customizing Views

ASP.NET MVC provides flexibility for styling and customizing Views:

a. Cascading Style Sheets (CSS): CSS can be used to define the visual appearance and layout of HTML elements within Views. By applying CSS classes and styles, you can create visually appealing and consistent user interfaces.

b. JavaScript and jQuery: You can enhance the interactivity of Views by adding JavaScript and leveraging jQuery, a popular JavaScript library. JavaScript enables dynamic behavior and client-side validations, while jQuery simplifies DOM manipulation and AJAX interactions.

c. View Models: View Models are custom classes that represent the data specifically required by a View. By using View Models, you can shape the data passed from the Controller to the View, ensuring that the View has exactly what it needs for rendering.

3.7 Summary

Understanding the MVC design pattern is crucial for successful ASP.NET MVC development. The clear separation of concerns and the ability to independently test, reuse, and extend components make ASP.NET MVC a powerful framework for building robust web applications.

Exercises:

1. Research and list three advantages of using the MVC pattern in web application development.

2. Describe the workflow of data and interactions in the MVC pattern.

3. Create a simple View using Razor syntax and experiment with adding dynamic data rendering.

Chapter 4: Creating Your First MVC Application

In this chapter, we will guide you through the process of creating your first MVC application. You will learn how to set up routes, create controllers, and implement actions to handle user requests.

4.1 Setting up Routes

Routes define the URL patterns and map them to specific controllers and actions in ASP.NET MVC. By configuring routes, you can create clean and search engine-friendly URLs. Let's set up a route for our application:

1. Open the `Startup.cs` file in your project.

2. Locate the `Configure` method.

3. Inside the `Configure` method, find the `UseEndpoints` section.

4. Add a new route using the `MapControllerRoute` method, providing a name, pattern, defaults, and optional parameters. Here's an example:

```csharp
app.UseEndpoints(endpoints =>

{

    endpoints.MapControllerRoute(
```

name: "default",

pattern: "{controller=Home}/{action=Index}/{id?}");

});

```
app.UseEndpoints(endpoints =>
{
    endpoints.MapControllerRoute(
        name: "default",
        pattern: "{controller=Home}/{action=Index}/{id?}");
});
```

In this example, the default route will map URLs like `/{controller}/{action}/{id}` to the corresponding controller and action. If no controller or action is specified, it will default to the `HomeController` and the `Index` action. The `id` parameter is optional.

4.2 Creating Controllers

Controllers handle user interactions, process requests, and coordinate the flow of data. Let's create our first controller:

1. In the Solution Explorer, right-click on the `Controllers` folder.

2. Select "Add" > "Controller".

3. In the "Add Scaffold" dialog, choose the "MVC Controller - Empty" option.

4. Provide a name for the controller, such as `HomeController`, and click "Add".

5. Visual Studio will generate a new controller class with the specified name.

Your new controller will look something like this:

```csharp
using Microsoft.AspNetCore.Mvc;


namespace YourApplication.Controllers
{
    public class HomeController : Controller
    {
        public IActionResult Index()
        {
            return View();
        }
    }
```

```
}
```

```
```

```
using Microsoft.AspNetCore.Mvc;

namespace YourApplication.Controllers
{
    public class HomeController : Controller
    {
        public IActionResult Index()
        {
            return View();
        }
    }
}
```

The `HomeController` class inherits from the `Controller` base class provided by ASP.NET MVC. It contains an `Index` action that returns a View.

4.3 Implementing Actions

Actions represent the individual operations that can be performed within a controller. Let's implement the `Index` action in our `HomeController`:

1. Open the `HomeController.cs` file.

2. Replace the existing `Index` method with the following code:

```csharp
public IActionResult Index()
{
    return View();
}
```

```
public IActionResult Index()
{
    return View();
}
```

In this example, the `Index` action returns a View. The View corresponds to a Razor template file that will be rendered when the action is invoked.

4.4 Creating Views

Views are responsible for presenting data to the user. Let's create a corresponding view for our `Index` action:

1. In the Solution Explorer, navigate to the `Views` folder.

2. Create a new folder named `Home`.

3. Inside the `Home` folder, add a new view file named `Index.cshtml`.

4. Open the `Index.cshtml` file and add the desired HTML and Razor code to define the UI for your page.

Here's a basic example of an `Index.cshtml` file:

```html
<h1>Welcome to My MVC Application</h1>
<p>This is the home page.</p>
```

```
<h1>Welcome to My MVC Application</h1>
<p>This is the home page.</p>
```

4.5 Testing Your Application

You are now ready to test your MVC application:

1. Build the project by selecting "Build" > "Build Solution" or pressing `Ctrl + Shift + B`.

2. Start the application by clicking the "Play" button or pressing `F5`.

3. Visual Studio will launch a web browser and navigate to the default URL of your application, such as `https://localhost:5001` or `http://localhost:5000`.

4. You should see the output of the `Index` action rendered in your browser.

Congratulations! You have successfully created your first MVC application in ASP.NET MVC. You set up routes, created a controller, implemented an action, and created a corresponding view.

Exercises:

1. Create a new controller named `AboutController` with an action named `Index`. Implement the action to return a view for the About page.

2. Add a new view file for the `AboutController`'s `Index` action. Customize the HTML content to display information about your application.

Chapter 5: Exploring the Project Structure

In this chapter, we will delve deeper into the project structure of an ASP.NET MVC application. Understanding the different folders and files will help you navigate and organize your code effectively.

5.1 Solution Structure Overview

Let's take a closer look at the typical structure of an ASP.NET MVC solution:

1. Solution File (.sln): The solution file serves as the container for your projects. It has the `.sln` extension and is created when you initially set up your solution in Visual Studio. It keeps track of all the projects within the solution.

2. Project: A project represents an individual application or component within a solution. In an ASP.NET MVC solution, you typically have the main MVC project, which contains the core application, and additional projects for other components such as class libraries, unit tests, or extensions.

3. Dependencies: The dependencies folder contains external libraries and NuGet packages that your project depends on. Visual Studio manages the dependencies and handles the retrieval and updating of packages.

4. Properties: The properties folder contains project-specific settings and configurations. It includes files like `launchSettings.json` that define how the application is launched and other project-related properties.

5. wwwroot: The wwwroot folder is the web root of your application. It contains static files such as CSS, JavaScript, images, and other assets that are directly served to clients. The web server considers this folder as the root when serving web content.

6. Controllers: The Controllers folder holds the controller classes. Controllers handle user interactions, process requests, and orchestrate the flow of data between models and views. Each controller typically corresponds to a specific area or functionality within the application.

7. Models: The Models folder contains the model classes that represent the application's data and business logic. Models are responsible for data access, validation, and behavior. They encapsulate the application's state and interact with data sources.

8. Views: The Views folder contains the view templates responsible for rendering the user interface. Views use the Razor syntax or other templating engines to generate dynamic HTML content. The Views folder typically mirrors the structure of the Controllers folder.

9. Migrations: If you are using Entity Framework for database access and have enabled migrations, the Migrations folder will contain the code files representing the database schema changes. These files are automatically created when you modify the database context or entity classes.

10. Startup.cs: The `Startup.cs` file contains the configuration for your application, including services, middleware, and routing configuration. It is the entry point for configuring your ASP.NET Core application.

5.2 Organizing Additional Files and Folders

Apart from the default folders mentioned above, you may create additional folders and files based on your project requirements. Here are some common practices for organizing additional files:

1. Services: You can create a separate folder to store service classes responsible for handling specific business logic or external integrations. This helps maintain a separation of concerns and keeps your codebase organized.

2. Helpers: If you have utility classes or helper methods that are used across your application, it is good practice to create a Helpers folder to store them. This improves code reuse and makes it easier to maintain and update common functionalities.

3. Extensions: If you develop custom extensions or reusable components, you can create an Extensions folder to contain those files. This way, you can easily locate and manage these extensions throughout your project.

4. Areas: If your application has distinct functional areas with their own set of controllers, models, and views, you can create separate folders for each area within the main project. This helps organize code related to specific areas of functionality.

5.3 Customizing View Locations

By default, ASP.NET MVC looks for views within the Views folder of your project. However, you can customize the view location to support different scenarios. Here's an example:

1. Open the `Startup.cs` file in your project.

2. Locate the `ConfigureServices` method.

3. Inside the `ConfigureServices` method, add the following code to customize view locations:

```csharp
services.Configure<RazorViewEngineOptions>(options =>
```

```
{

    options.ViewLocationFormats.Clear();

    options.ViewLocationFormats.Add("/CustomViews/{1}/{0}" +
RazorViewEngine.ViewExtension);

    options.ViewLocationFormats.Add("/CustomViews/Shared/{0}" +
RazorViewEngine.ViewExtension);

});

```

```
services.Configure<RazorViewEngineOptions>(options =>
{
    options.ViewLocationFormats.Clear();
    options.ViewLocationFormats.Add("/CustomViews/{1}/{0}" + RazorViewEngine.ViewExtension);
    options.ViewLocationFormats.Add("/CustomViews/Shared/{0}" + RazorViewEngine.ViewExtension);
});
```

In this example, we specify custom view locations. The first line
clears the default view locations, and the subsequent lines add new
locations. Here, we specify that views can be found in the
`/CustomViews` folder and its subfolders. Additionally, we specify a
shared folder within the `CustomViews` folder for shared views.

5.4 Summary

Understanding the project structure of an ASP.NET MVC application
is vital for organizing and maintaining your codebase effectively. Each
folder and file serves a specific purpose, facilitating separation of
concerns and ensuring scalability and maintainability.

Exercises:

1. Create a new folder named `Services` in your project and move any relevant service classes into this folder.

2. Customize the view location to look for views in a different folder and verify that it works as expected.

3. Familiarize yourself with the existing files and folders in your ASP.NET MVC project and identify their respective purposes.

Great job completing Day 5! Tomorrow, we will explore working with data and Entity Framework in ASP.NET MVC.

Day 2:
Building the Model

Welcome to Day 2 of your journey to learn ASP.NET MVC! In this chapter, we will explore the concept of models in ASP.NET MVC and their role in building web applications.

Chapter 1: Understanding Models in ASP.NET MVC

21.1 What are Models in ASP.NET MVC?

In ASP.NET MVC, models represent the application's data and encapsulate the business logic related to that data. They are responsible for managing the application's state, performing data operations, and providing data to the views for presentation.

Models in ASP.NET MVC are typically implemented as classes. These classes define the structure and behavior of the data, including properties, methods, and relationships with other models.

1.2 Responsibilities of Models

Models in ASP.NET MVC have several key responsibilities:

- Data Access: Models interact with the underlying data sources, such as databases or web services, to perform CRUD (Create, Read, Update, Delete) operations. They encapsulate the logic for querying, inserting, updating, and deleting data.

- Data Validation: Models enforce data validation rules to ensure the integrity and consistency of the data. They define validation constraints, such as required fields, data types, length limits, and custom validation rules.

- Business Logic: Models encapsulate the business rules and logic related to the data. They implement calculations, transformations, and other operations that are specific to the application's domain.

1.3 Implementing Models in ASP.NET MVC

To create a model in ASP.NET MVC, you typically define a class that represents a specific entity or concept in your application. This class will have properties that correspond to the attributes or fields of the entity.

Here's an example of a simple model class representing a "Product":

```csharp
public class Product
{
    public int Id { get; set; }

    public string Name { get; set; }

    public decimal Price { get; set; }

    public DateTime CreatedAt { get; set; }
```

```
}

```

```
public class Product
{
    public int Id { get; set; }
    public string Name { get; set; }
    public decimal Price { get; set; }
    public DateTime CreatedAt { get; set; }
}
```

In this example, the `Product` class has properties to store the product's ID, name, price, and creation date. These properties provide a structure to hold the data and can be accessed or modified by other components in the application.

1.4 Data Annotations and Validation in Models

ASP.NET MVC provides data annotations that you can apply to model properties to enforce data validation rules. These annotations allow you to declaratively specify validation constraints and provide a convenient way to define validation rules directly within the model class.

Here are some commonly used data annotations:

- `[Required]`: Specifies that a property is required and must have a value.

- `[StringLength(maximumLength)]`: Sets the maximum length allowed for a string property.

- `[Range(minimum, maximum)]`: Defines a range constraint for numeric properties.

- `[RegularExpression(pattern)]`: Specifies a regular expression pattern that a string property must match.

- `[EmailAddress]`: Validates that a string property contains a valid email address.

By applying data annotations to model properties, you can ensure that the data entered by users meets the required criteria.

1.5 Testing Models

Testing models is an important part of ensuring the correctness and reliability of your application. Unit testing frameworks, such as NUnit or xUnit, can be used to write automated tests for your models.

You can create test cases to validate various aspects of your models, such as data validation rules, business logic, and interactions with data sources. By testing your models, you can catch bugs early, ensure data integrity, and maintain the overall quality of your application.

1.6 Summary

Models play a crucial role in ASP.NET MVC development as they represent the data and encapsulate the business logic of an application. Understanding how to implement models, apply data annotations for validation, and test models is essential for building robust and reliable ASP.NET MVC applications.

Exercises:

1. Create a model class for a "Customer" with properties such as ID, Name, Email, and Phone.

2. Apply data annotations to the properties of the "Customer" model to enforce validation rules.

3. Write a unit test to validate the behavior of a specific method in one of your model classes.

Chapter 2: Creating Model Classes

In this chapter, we will focus on creating model classes in ASP.NET MVC. Model classes represent the data and business logic of your application, and they play a vital role in building robust web applications.

2.1 Understanding Model Classes

In ASP.NET MVC, model classes define the structure and behavior of the data entities in your application. They encapsulate the properties and methods that represent the attributes and operations related to the data.

Model classes are typically implemented as C# or VB.NET classes. These classes can contain properties, methods, and other members that define the behavior and structure of the data.

2.2 Creating a Model Class

To create a model class in ASP.NET MVC, follow these steps:

1. Open your project in Visual Studio.

2. Right-click on the project in the Solution Explorer and select "Add" -> "Class."

3. Name the class and choose a suitable name that reflects the entity or concept it represents. For example, if you are creating a model for a "Product," name the class "Product.cs" or a more descriptive name.

4. In the class file, define the properties that represent the attributes of the entity. For example:

```csharp
public class Product
{
    public int Id { get; set; }

    public string Name { get; set; }

    public decimal Price { get; set; }

    public DateTime CreatedAt { get; set; }
}
```

```csharp
public class Product
{
    public int Id { get; set; }
    public string Name { get; set; }
    public decimal Price { get; set; }
    public DateTime CreatedAt { get; set; }
}
```

In this example, the `Product` class represents a product entity with properties for its ID, name, price, and creation date. Each property has a getter and a setter (`get; set;`) to allow access to and modification of the data.

2.3 Adding Additional Members to the Model Class

Model classes can contain additional members such as methods, constructors, and custom validation logic. You can define methods that perform calculations or implement specific business logic associated with the entity.

For example, you can add a method to calculate the total price of a product:

```csharp
public decimal CalculateTotalPrice()
{
    return Price * Quantity;
```

```
}
```

```
```

```
public decimal CalculateTotalPrice()
{
    return Price * Quantity;
}
```

In this example, the `CalculateTotalPrice` method multiplies the price of the product by its quantity to calculate the total price.

2.4 Relationships between Model Classes

In many applications, entities have relationships with each other. For example, a "Customer" entity may have multiple "Order" entities associated with it. In such cases, you can define relationships between model classes.

There are different types of relationships, such as one-to-one, one-to-many, and many-to-many. You can establish these relationships by adding navigation properties to your model classes.

For example, consider the following model classes representing a one-to-many relationship between "Author" and "Book":

_**

```csharp
```

```csharp
public class Author
{
    public int Id { get; set; }
    public string Name { get; set; }


    public ICollection<Book> Books { get; set; }
}


public class Book
{
    public int Id { get; set; }
    public string Title { get; set; }


    public int AuthorId { get; set; }
    public Author Author { get; set; }
}
```

```
public class Author
{
    public int Id { get; set; }
    public string Name { get; set; }

    public ICollection<Book> Books { get; set; }
}

public class Book
{
    public int Id { get; set; }
    public string Title { get; set; }

    public int AuthorId { get; set; }
    public Author Author { get; set; }
}
```

In this example, the `Author` class has a collection of `Book` entities associated with it through the `Books` property. The `Book` class has an `AuthorId` property and an `Author` navigation property representing the relationship to the `Author` entity.

2.5 Summary

Model classes are the foundation of your ASP.NET MVC application. They define the structure and behavior of the data entities in your application and encapsulate the business logic. By creating model classes, you can represent the data accurately and handle operations associated with it.

Exercises:

1. Create a model class for a "Customer" entity with properties such as ID, Name, Email, and Phone.

2. Add a method to the "Customer" model class to calculate the customer's age based on their birthdate.

3. Create model classes for two related entities in your application and define the appropriate relationships between them.

Chapter 3: Implementing Data Access with Entity Framework

In this chapter, we will focus on implementing data access using Entity Framework in ASP.NET MVC.

3.1 Understanding Entity Framework

Entity Framework (EF) is an Object-Relational Mapping (ORM) framework provided by Microsoft. It enables you to work with relational databases using object-oriented concepts, making data access easier and more efficient.

EF provides a set of tools and libraries that allow you to define your data model using classes and properties. It then takes care of mapping these classes and properties to database tables and columns, allowing you to interact with the database using object-oriented code.

3.2 Setting up Entity Framework

To use Entity Framework in your ASP.NET MVC application, you need to set it up and configure it. Here are the steps:

1. Install Entity Framework: In Visual Studio, right-click on your project in the Solution Explorer, select "Manage NuGet Packages,"

and search for "EntityFramework." Install the latest version of Entity Framework.

2. Create a DbContext Class: A DbContext class represents the database context and acts as the main entry point for working with the database. Create a new class that derives from the `DbContext` class and defines the data sets (DbSet) for your model classes.

```csharp
public class ApplicationDbContext : DbContext

{

    public DbSet<Product> Products { get; set; }

    public DbSet<Customer> Customers { get; set; }

}
```

```
public class ApplicationDbContext : DbContext
{
    public DbSet<Product> Products { get; set; }
    public DbSet<Customer> Customers { get; set; }
}
```

In this example, `ApplicationDbContext` is the database context class that exposes two `DbSet` properties for the `Product` and `Customer` model classes.

3. Configure Connection String: Open the `Web.config` or `App.config` file in your project and add a connection string that points to your database. Specify the connection string name in the constructor of your `DbContext` class.

```xml
<connectionStrings>

  <add name="DefaultConnection" connectionString="Data Source=(LocalDb)\MSSQLLocalDB;Database=YourDatabase;Integrated Security=True" providerName="System.Data.SqlClient" />

</connectionStrings>
```

```
<connectionStrings>
    <add name="DefaultConnection" connectionString="Data Source=(LocalDb)\MSSQLLocalDB;Database
        =YourDatabase;Integrated Security=True" providerName="System.Data.SqlClient" />
</connectionStrings>
```

4. Enable Migrations: Entity Framework uses migrations to manage database changes over time. Open the Package Manager Console in Visual Studio (`Tools` -> `NuGet Package Manager` -> `Package Manager Console`) and run the following command:

```

Enable-Migrations
```

```
Enable-Migrations
```

This command initializes the migrations configuration in your project.

5. Create Initial Migration: Run the following command in the Package Manager Console to create an initial migration:

```
```

Add-Migration InitialCreate

```
```

```
Add-Migration InitialCreate
```

This command creates a migration file that represents the initial state of your database.

6. Update Database: Finally, run the following command to apply the migration and update the database:

```
```

Update-Database

```
```

```
Update-Database
```

This command applies the pending migrations to the database and creates the necessary tables and columns based on your model classes.

3.3 Performing Data Operations

With Entity Framework set up, you can now perform data operations using the DbContext and model classes. Entity Framework provides methods for querying, inserting, updating, and deleting data.

Here's an example of querying products from the database using Entity Framework:

```csharp
using (var context = new ApplicationDbContext())
{
    var products = context.Products.ToList();

    // Use the products...

}
```

```
using (var context = new ApplicationDbContext())
{
    var products = context.Products.ToList();
    // Use the products...
}
```

In this example, we create an instance of the `ApplicationDbContext` and use the `Products` property to access the products table in the database.

You can also perform other data operations like inserting, updating, and deleting records using Entity Framework's methods and LINQ queries.

3.4 Summary

Entity Framework is a powerful ORM framework that simplifies data access in ASP.NET MVC applications. By setting up Entity Framework and configuring a DbContext class, you can leverage its capabilities to interact with the database using object-oriented code.

Exercises:

1. Install Entity Framework using NuGet package manager in your ASP.NET MVC project.

2. Create a DbContext class and define the necessary DbSet properties for your model classes.

3. Use Entity Framework to query data from the database and perform CRUD operations.

Chapter 4: Working with Data Annotations and Validation

In this chapter, we will focus on working with data annotations and validation in ASP.NET MVC.

4.1 Understanding Data Annotations

Data annotations are attributes that you can apply to model properties to define validation rules and provide metadata for data display and formatting. ASP.NET MVC uses data annotations to perform server-side validation, generate client-side validation scripts, and customize the display of data.

4.2 Commonly Used Data Annotations

Here are some commonly used data annotations in ASP.NET MVC:

- `[Required]`: Specifies that a property is required and must have a value.

- `[StringLength(maximumLength)]`: Sets the maximum length allowed for a string property.

- `[Range(minimum, maximum)]`: Defines a range constraint for numeric properties.

- `[RegularExpression(pattern)]`: Specifies a regular expression pattern that a string property must match.

- `[EmailAddress]`: Validates that a string property contains a valid email address.

- `[Compare(otherProperty)]`: Compares the value of a property with another property.

These annotations provide a declarative way to define validation rules for your model properties.

4.3 Applying Data Annotations

To apply data annotations to model properties, simply add the desired annotation attribute above the corresponding property. Here's an example:

```csharp
public class Product
{
    public int Id { get; set; }
```

```
[Required]

public string Name { get; set; }


[Range(0, 1000)]

public decimal Price { get; set; }


[EmailAddress]

public string Email { get; set; }
}
```

```
public class Product
{
    public int Id { get; set; }

    [Required]
    public string Name { get; set; }

    [Range(0, 1000)]
    public decimal Price { get; set; }

    [EmailAddress]
    public string Email { get; set; }
}
```

In this example, the `Name` property is marked as `[Required]`, ensuring that it must have a value. The `Price` property has a `[Range]` annotation, limiting its value between 0 and 1000. The

`Email` property has the `[EmailAddress]` annotation, validating that it contains a valid email address.

4.4 Validation in ASP.NET MVC

ASP.NET MVC automatically performs server-side validation based on the data annotations applied to model properties. If any validation rule fails, the model state becomes invalid, and you can display error messages to the user.

To validate the model and check its state, you can use the `ModelState.IsValid` property. Here's an example:

```csharp
[HttpPost]

public ActionResult Create(Product product)

{

    if (ModelState.IsValid)

    {

        // Save the product to the database

        // Redirect to the success page

    }
```

// Model state is invalid, redisplay the form with error messages

return View(product);

}

```
[HttpPost]
public ActionResult Create(Product product)
{
    if (ModelState.IsValid)
    {
        // Save the product to the database
        // Redirect to the success page
    }

    // Model state is invalid, redisplay the form with error messages
    return View(product);
}
```

In this example, the `Create` action method receives a `Product` object as a parameter. It checks if the model state is valid using `ModelState.IsValid`. If it is valid, the product is saved to the database. Otherwise, the form is redisplayed with error messages.

4.5 Custom Validation

In addition to the built-in data annotations, you can also create custom validation rules by implementing the `ValidationAttribute` class. This allows you to define custom logic to validate properties based on your specific requirements.

Here's an example of a custom validation attribute:

```csharp

public class CustomValidationAttribute : ValidationAttribute

{

    protected override ValidationResult IsValid(object value,
ValidationContext validationContext)

    {

        // Custom validation logic goes here

        // Return ValidationResult.Success for valid values

        // Return new ValidationResult(ErrorMessage) for invalid values

    }

}
```

```
public class CustomValidationAttribute : ValidationAttribute
{
    protected override ValidationResult IsValid(object value, ValidationContext validationContext)
    {
        // Custom validation logic goes here
        // Return ValidationResult.Success for valid values
        // Return new ValidationResult(ErrorMessage) for invalid values
    }
}
```

You can then apply this custom validation attribute to your model properties.

4.6 Summary

Data annotations provide a convenient way to define validation rules and metadata for model properties in ASP.NET MVC. By applying data annotations, you can perform server-side validation, generate client-side validation scripts, and customize the display and formatting of data.

Exercises:

1. Apply data annotations to the properties of your model classes to enforce validation rules.

2. Implement custom validation logic for a specific property using a custom validation attribute.

3. Test the validation by submitting data to your application and verifying the error messages.

Chapter 5: Testing Model Classes

5.1 Importance of Testing Model Classes

Testing model classes is crucial for ensuring the correctness and reliability of your application's data and business logic. By writing tests for your model classes, you can validate their behavior, catch bugs early, and ensure that they perform as expected.

5.2 Unit Testing Model Classes

Unit testing is a popular approach for testing individual components of an application. It involves writing small, isolated tests that verify the behavior of a specific unit of code, such as a method or a class.

To perform unit testing on your model classes in ASP.NET MVC, follow these steps:

1. Create a Test Project: In Visual Studio, create a new test project within your solution. You can choose a unit testing framework like NUnit or xUnit.NET.

2. Write Test Methods: Create test methods that cover different scenarios and aspects of your model classes. For example, you can write tests to validate the behavior of methods, test edge cases, and verify that validation rules are enforced.

3. Set Up Test Data: In each test method, set up the necessary test data to simulate different scenarios. This may involve creating instances of your model classes, setting property values, and configuring the state of the objects.

4. Execute Tests: Run the tests and verify that the model classes behave as expected. Use assertions to validate the results and compare them against the expected outcomes.

5.3 Testing Example

Here's an example of a unit test for a model class:

```csharp
[TestFixture]

public class ProductTests

{

    [Test]

    public void CalculateTotalPrice_ShouldReturnCorrectValue()

    {

        // Arrange

        var product = new Product { Price = 10.0m, Quantity = 5 };
```

// Act

var total = product.CalculateTotalPrice();

// Assert

Assert.AreEqual(50.0m, total);

  }

}

```

```

```csharp
[TestFixture]
public class ProductTests
{
    [Test]
    public void CalculateTotalPrice_ShouldReturnCorrectValue()
    {
        // Arrange
        var product = new Product { Price = 10.0m, Quantity = 5 };

        // Act
        var total = product.CalculateTotalPrice();

        // Assert
        Assert.AreEqual(50.0m, total);
    }
}
```

In this example, we have a test method that verifies the correctness of the `CalculateTotalPrice` method in the `Product` class. We create an instance of the `Product` class, set the price and quantity, call the method, and assert that the calculated total matches the expected value.

5.4 Benefits of Testing Model Classes

Testing model classes in ASP.NET MVC offers several benefits:

- Bug Detection: Tests help catch bugs and issues in your model classes early in the development process, making it easier to identify and fix problems.

- Reliability: By testing different scenarios and edge cases, you can ensure that your model classes behave consistently and reliably.

- Maintainability: Tests act as documentation for your model classes, providing a clear understanding of their expected behavior. They also make it easier to refactor or modify the code with confidence.

- Regression Testing: Tests act as a safety net to ensure that changes to your model classes don't introduce new bugs or regressions.

5.5 Summary

Testing model classes in ASP.NET MVC is essential for validating their behavior, ensuring reliability, and catching bugs early. Unit testing provides a structured approach to testing individual components of your application, such as model methods and properties.

In the next chapter, we will delve into developing views in ASP.NET MVC. We will explore the creation of view templates using Razor syntax, working with layouts and partial views, and implementing forms and HTML helpers.

Exercises:

1. Set up a test project in your solution for testing model classes.

2. Write unit tests to verify the behavior of methods or properties in your model classes.

3. Run the tests and ensure they pass successfully.

Great job completing Day 2! Tomorrow, we will delve into developing views in ASP.NET MVC.

Day 3: Developing the Views

Welcome to Day 3 of your journey to learn ASP.NET MVC! In this chapter, we will introduce views in ASP.NET MVC and discuss their importance in building web applications.

Chapter 1: Introduction to Views in ASP.NET MVC

1.1 What are Views in ASP.NET MVC?

In ASP.NET MVC, views are responsible for presenting the user interface of your application. They define the structure, layout, and appearance of the content that is rendered and displayed to the user.

Views are typically created using markup languages like HTML, combined with server-side code to dynamically generate content. ASP.NET MVC uses a view engine, such as Razor, to blend HTML markup with server-side code seamlessly.

1.2 Role of Views in MVC Architecture

In the Model-View-Controller (MVC) architecture, views are one of the three main components. Their primary role is to present the data provided by the model to the user in a visually appealing and interactive manner.

Views are decoupled from the business logic and data manipulation, allowing for a clear separation of concerns. They receive data from the controller, format it appropriately, and render it to the user.

1.3 Creating Views in ASP.NET MVC

To create a view in ASP.NET MVC, follow these steps:

1. Open your project in Visual Studio.

2. Locate the `Views` folder within your project's structure.

3. Within the `Views` folder, create a subfolder that corresponds to the controller for which you are creating the view. For example, if you have a `HomeController`, create a folder named `Home` within the `Views` folder.

4. Inside the controller-specific folder, create a view file with the appropriate extension (e.g., `.cshtml` for Razor views).

5. In the view file, write the HTML markup that represents the user interface of your application. You can embed server-side code using Razor syntax to incorporate dynamic content and logic.

1.4 Rendering Views from Controllers

Views are rendered and displayed to the user by the controller. The controller retrieves data from the model and passes it to the appropriate view for rendering. The rendered view is then sent back to the user's browser as the response.

To render a view from a controller action, you typically use the `View` method and pass it the desired view name. For example:

```csharp
public ActionResult Index()
{
    var data = // retrieve data from the model
    return View("Index", data);
}
```

```
public ActionResult Index()
{
    var data = // retrieve data from the model
    return View("Index", data);
}
```

In this example, the `Index` action method retrieves data from the model and passes it to the `Index` view for rendering.

1.5 Summary

Views are an integral part of ASP.NET MVC development. They provide the user interface for your application, presenting data to the user in a visually appealing and interactive manner. Views are decoupled from the business logic and data manipulation, allowing for a clear separation of concerns in the MVC architecture.

Exercises:

1. Create a view file for one of the controller actions in your ASP.NET MVC application.

2. Render the view from the corresponding controller action and test its functionality.

3. Customize the appearance of the view by modifying the HTML markup.

Chapter 2: Creating View Templates using Razor Syntax

In this chapter, we will delve into creating view templates using Razor syntax. Razor is the default view engine in ASP.NET MVC, providing a concise and powerful syntax for combining HTML markup with server-side code.

2.1 Understanding Razor Syntax

Razor syntax allows you to embed server-side code directly within your view templates. It provides a seamless way to mix HTML markup with server-side code, making it easier to generate dynamic content and interact with data.

Razor syntax uses special markers, such as `@`, to identify server-side code blocks or expressions. These markers differentiate between HTML markup and server-side code, allowing you to switch between the two seamlessly.

2.2 Basic Razor Syntax

Let's explore some basic Razor syntax examples:

- Embedding Server-Side Code:

```html
```

```
<p>Welcome, @User.Name!</p>
```

```
<p>Welcome, @User.Name!</p>
```

In this example, the `User.Name` property is rendered dynamically within the HTML paragraph.

- Conditionals:

```html
@if (User.IsAuthenticated)

{

    <p>Welcome, @User.Name!</p>

}

else

{

    <p>Please log in to access the content.</p>

}
```

```
@if (User.IsAuthenticated)
{
    <p>Welcome, @User.Name!</p>
}
else
{
    <p>Please log in to access the content.</p>
}
```

This example demonstrates conditional rendering based on the user's authentication status.

- Loops:

```html
<ul>
    @foreach (var item in Model.Items)
    {
        <li>@item.Name</li>
    }
</ul>
```

```
<ul>
    @foreach (var item in Model.Items)
    {
        <li>@item.Name</li>
    }
</ul>
```

Here, the `foreach` loop iterates over the `Model.Items` collection and dynamically generates list items based on the data.

2.3 Layouts and Sections

Razor syntax also provides support for layouts and sections. Layouts allow you to define a common structure for multiple views, reducing redundancy in your code. Sections enable you to define placeholders in your layout where specific content can be injected from individual views.

- Defining a Layout:

To define a layout, create a layout file with the `.cshtml` extension. Within the layout, use the `@RenderBody` marker to indicate where the content from the individual views should be inserted.

- Injecting Content into Sections:

Within your individual views, use the `@section` directive to define sections and provide the specific content to be injected into those sections.

2.4 HTML Helpers

Razor syntax includes HTML helpers that simplify the generation of HTML elements and reduce the amount of manual HTML coding. These helpers generate HTML markup dynamically based on the provided parameters.

For example, the `Html.ActionLink` helper generates an HTML hyperlink for navigating to different actions within your application:

```html
@Html.ActionLink("Home", "Index", "Home")
```

```
@Html.ActionLink("Home", "Index", "Home")
```

2.5 Summary

Razor syntax is a powerful tool for creating view templates in ASP.NET MVC. It allows you to seamlessly blend HTML markup with server-side code, enabling the generation of dynamic content and interaction with data. Razor syntax supports conditionals, loops, layouts, sections, and HTML helpers to simplify view template development.

Exercises:

1. Update one of your view templates to use Razor syntax for dynamic content rendering.

2. Create a layout file and configure your views to use the layout.

3. Use HTML helpers to generate HTML elements in your view templates.

Chapter 3: Working with Layouts and Partial Views

In this chapter, we will explore layouts and partial views in ASP.NET MVC. Layouts provide a consistent structure for your views, while partial views allow you to reuse and modularize specific sections of your views.

3.1 Understanding Layouts

Layouts in ASP.NET MVC are used to define a common structure for multiple views. They help maintain a consistent UI design and reduce redundancy by separating the common layout elements from the view-specific content.

A layout typically includes the HTML structure, header, footer, navigation menus, and any other shared components that should appear on multiple views.

3.2 Creating a Layout

To create a layout in ASP.NET MVC, follow these steps:

1. Create a layout file with the `.cshtml` extension. For example, you can name it `_Layout.cshtml`.

2. Define the HTML structure, header, footer, navigation menus, and any other shared components within the layout file.

3. Use the `@RenderBody` marker within the layout file to indicate where the content from individual views should be inserted.

4. Specify the layout for each view by adding the `Layout` directive at the top of the view file. For example:

```html
@{
    Layout = "_Layout";
}
```

```
@{
    Layout = "_Layout";
}
```

By specifying the layout for a view, the content of that view will be rendered within the defined layout structure.

3.3 Working with Partial Views

Partial views allow you to reuse and modularize specific sections of your views. They are similar to regular views but are intended to be embedded within other views or layout files.

Partial views are useful for creating reusable components, such as navigation menus, sidebars, or widgets, that can be rendered across multiple views.

To create a partial view, follow these steps:

1. Create a view file with the `.cshtml` extension. For example, you can name it `_PartialView.cshtml`.

2. Define the content specific to the partial view within the file.

3. Render the partial view within another view or layout file using the `Partial` method. For example:

```html
@Html.Partial("_PartialView")
```

```
@Html.Partial("_PartialView")
```

By rendering the partial view, its content will be embedded within the parent view or layout.

3.4 Passing Data to Partial Views

Partial views can also receive data from the parent view or layout. You can pass data using the `@model` directive and access it within the partial view using the `Model` property.

Here's an example of passing data to a partial view:

Parent View:

```html
@{
    var data = new List<string> { "Item 1", "Item 2", "Item 3" };
}

@Html.Partial("_PartialView", data)
```

```
@{
    var data = new List<string> { "Item 1", "Item 2", "Item 3" };
}
@Html.Partial("_PartialView", data)
```

Partial View:

```html
@model IEnumerable<string>


<ul>
  @foreach (var item in Model)
  {
    <li>@item</li>
  }
</ul>
```

```
@model IEnumerable<string>

<ul>
    @foreach (var item in Model)
    {
        <li>@item</li>
    }
</ul>
```

In this example, the parent view passes a list of strings to the partial view, which iterates over the items and renders them as list items.

3.5 Summary

Layouts and partial views are valuable tools for organizing and reusing code in ASP.NET MVC. Layouts provide a consistent structure for multiple views, while partial views allow you to modularize and reuse specific sections of your views. By utilizing layouts and partial views effectively, you can maintain a consistent UI design, reduce redundancy, and improve code maintainability.

Exercises:

1. Create a layout file and define the common structure and components for your views.

2. Implement a partial view for a reusable component within your application.

3. Pass data from a parent view to a partial view and render the data dynamically.

Chapter 4: Implementing Forms and HTML Helpers

In this chapter, we will focus on implementing forms and using HTML helpers in ASP.NET MVC. Forms allow users to input and submit data, while HTML helpers simplify the generation of HTML elements and form controls.

4.1 Creating Forms in ASP.NET MVC

Forms play a crucial role in web applications as they allow users to interact with and submit data. In ASP.NET MVC, you can create forms using HTML markup and utilize the features provided by the framework to handle form submissions and validation.

To create a form in ASP.NET MVC, follow these steps:

1. Begin the form using the `Html.BeginForm` method. Specify the action method and controller that will handle the form submission.

```html
@using (Html.BeginForm("ActionMethod", "Controller",
FormMethod.Post))

{

   // Form content goes here
```

```
    // Input fields, buttons, etc.

}

```
```
@using (Html.BeginForm("ActionMethod", "Controller", FormMethod.Post))
{
    // Form content goes here
    // Input fields, buttons, etc.
}
```

2. Add form controls within the form using HTML markup. Use appropriate input elements, such as `input`, `select`, `textarea`, and apply necessary attributes for validation, like `required`, `maxlength`, etc.

3. Add a submit button to allow users to submit the form data.

4. Handle the form submission in the specified action method of the controller.

4.2 Working with HTML Helpers

HTML helpers in ASP.NET MVC simplify the generation of HTML elements and form controls. They provide a convenient way to generate HTML markup based on the provided parameters, reducing the amount of manual HTML coding.

Some commonly used HTML helpers include:

- `Html.TextBoxFor`: Generates an HTML text input field.

- `Html.DropDownListFor`: Generates an HTML dropdown list.

- `Html.CheckBoxFor`: Generates an HTML checkbox input field.

- `Html.TextAreaFor`: Generates an HTML textarea element.

These helpers automatically handle binding the input values with the corresponding model properties.

Example usage of an HTML helper:

```html
@Html.TextBoxFor(model => model.Name)
```

```
@Html.TextBoxFor(model => model.Name)
```

In this example, the `TextBoxFor` helper generates an HTML text input field based on the `Name` property of the model.

4.3 Handling Form Submissions

To handle form submissions, you need to create an action method in the controller that corresponds to the form's action attribute. The action method should have the `HttpPost` attribute and accept the form data as parameters.

Example of a form submission handling action method:

```csharp
[HttpPost]

public ActionResult SubmitForm(FormModel formData)

{

    // Process the submitted form data

    // Perform validation, save data to the database, etc.

    return RedirectToAction("Success");

}
```

```
[HttpPost]
public ActionResult SubmitForm(FormModel formData)
{
    // Process the submitted form data
    // Perform validation, save data to the database, etc.

    return RedirectToAction("Success");
}
```

In this example, the `SubmitForm` action method receives the submitted form data in a model object named `FormModel`. You can process the data, perform validation, and take appropriate actions.

4.4 Summary

Forms and HTML helpers are essential elements in building interactive and data-driven views in ASP.NET MVC. By creating forms, handling form submissions, and utilizing HTML helpers, you can simplify the process of creating and managing user input.

Exercises:

1. Create a form in one of your views using the `Html.BeginForm` method.

2. Use HTML helpers to generate form controls within the form.

3. Implement the corresponding action method in the controller to handle the form submission.

Chapter 5: Styling and Customizing Views

In this chapter, we will explore various techniques for styling and customizing views in ASP.NET MVC. Customizing the visual appearance of your views is crucial for creating a compelling user experience.

5.1 CSS Styling

CSS (Cascading Style Sheets) is a powerful tool for styling your views in ASP.NET MVC. CSS allows you to control the layout, colors, fonts, and other visual aspects of your HTML elements.

To apply CSS styles to your views, follow these steps:

1. Create a CSS file or use an existing one. You can place the CSS file in a folder within your project, such as `Content` or `wwwroot`.

2. Link the CSS file to your views by including the following code in the `<head>` section of your layout file or individual views:

```html
<link rel="stylesheet" type="text/css"
href="path/to/your/css/file.css" />
```

```
`` `
```

```
<link rel="stylesheet" type="text/css" href="path/to/your/css/file.css" />
```

Make sure to replace `"path/to/your/css/file.css"` with the actual path to your CSS file.

3. Define CSS rules in your CSS file to target specific HTML elements, classes, or IDs and apply the desired styles. For example:

```css
h1 {

    color: #333;

    font-size: 24px;

}


.my-class {

    background-color: #f2f2f2;

    padding: 10px;

}


#my-id {
```

```
        font-weight: bold;

}

```

```css
h1 {
    color: #333;
    font-size: 24px;
}

.my-class {
    background-color: #f2f2f2;
    padding: 10px;
}

#my-id {
    font-weight: bold;
}
```

In this example, the CSS rules target `<h1>` elements, elements with the class `.my-class`, and the element with the ID `#my-id`.

5.2 Bootstrap Framework

Bootstrap is a popular CSS framework that provides a set of pre-designed CSS styles and components. It offers a responsive grid system, typography, forms, buttons, and other UI elements that can be easily integrated into your ASP.NET MVC views.

To use Bootstrap in your ASP.NET MVC project, follow these steps:

1. Install Bootstrap: You can install Bootstrap by including the Bootstrap CSS and JavaScript files in your project. You can use a package manager like NuGet or download the files from the official Bootstrap website.

2. Link Bootstrap in your views: Include the Bootstrap CSS file in your layout or individual views using the `<link>` tag. You can also include the Bootstrap JavaScript file for interactive components like dropdown menus or modals.

```html
<link rel="stylesheet"
href="path/to/bootstrap/css/bootstrap.min.css" />

<script src="path/to/bootstrap/js/bootstrap.min.js"></script>
```

```
<link rel="stylesheet" href="path/to/bootstrap/css/bootstrap.min.css" />
<script src="path/to/bootstrap/js/bootstrap.min.js"></script>
```

3. Utilize Bootstrap classes and components: Bootstrap provides a wide range of CSS classes and components that you can use to style your HTML elements. Refer to the Bootstrap documentation to explore the available options and examples.

5.3 Customizing Views with Razor Syntax

Razor syntax allows you to dynamically generate HTML and apply customizations based on the server-side logic. You can leverage Razor syntax to conditionally apply CSS classes, set inline styles, or customize the HTML structure of your views.

Here's an example of using Razor syntax to apply a CSS class conditionally:

```html
<div class="@(Model.IsActive ? "active" : "")">
    Content here
</div>
```

```
<div class="@(Model.IsActive ? "active" : "")">
    Content here
</div>
```

In this example, the CSS class `"active"` is applied to the `<div>` element based on the value of the `IsActive` property of the model.

5.4 Summary

Styling and customizing views is an essential aspect of creating visually appealing and user-friendly applications. By applying CSS styles, utilizing frameworks like Bootstrap, and leveraging Razor syntax for dynamic customizations, you can create engaging and personalized views in ASP.NET MVC..

Exercises:

1. Create a CSS file and apply custom styles to your views.

2. Explore the Bootstrap framework and integrate it into your ASP.NET MVC views.

3. Use Razor syntax to conditionally apply CSS classes or customize the HTML structure in your views.

Day 4: Controllers and Routing

Welcome to Day 4 of your journey to learn ASP.NET MVC! In this chapter, we will explore controllers in ASP.NET MVC and understand their role in handling user requests and coordinating the flow of data between the model and views.

Chapter 1: Introduction to Controllers

1.1 What are Controllers?

Controllers in ASP.NET MVC are responsible for handling user requests, processing data, and determining the appropriate response to send back to the user. They act as an intermediary between the model (data) and the views (user interface).

Controllers contain action methods that are invoked in response to user requests. These action methods receive input from the user, interact with the model to retrieve or manipulate data, and pass the data to the appropriate views for rendering.

1.2 Creating Controllers

To create a controller in ASP.NET MVC, follow these steps:

1. In your project, locate the `Controllers` folder.

2. Right-click on the `Controllers` folder and choose "Add" -> "Controller" from the context menu.

3. Select the appropriate template for your controller, such as "Empty Controller" or "Controller with Read/Write Actions."

4. Provide a name for your controller and click "Add."

This will create a new controller file with a corresponding class and default action methods.

1.3 Anatomy of a Controller

A typical controller in ASP.NET MVC consists of the following components:

- Controller class: This is a C# class that derives from the `Controller` base class provided by the framework. It contains action methods and other supporting methods.

- Action methods: These methods are responsible for processing user requests and returning responses. Each action method represents a specific action that the user can perform.

- Attributes: Attributes can be applied to the controller or action methods to define additional behaviors or constraints, such as authorization, caching, or HTTP verb constraints.

1.4 Handling User Requests

Controllers handle user requests by mapping the incoming requests to specific action methods. The routing mechanism in ASP.NET MVC determines which controller and action method should be invoked based on the URL and route configuration.

To handle a user request, the controller class must have an action method with the appropriate signature and the `[HttpGet]` attribute (unless it handles a different HTTP verb).

Here's an example of an action method that handles a GET request:

```csharp
public ActionResult Index()
{
    // Retrieve data from the model

    // Perform any necessary processing

    // Pass data to the view for rendering

    return View();
}
```

```
public ActionResult Index()
{
    // Retrieve data from the model
    // Perform any necessary processing
    // Pass data to the view for rendering

    return View();
}
```

In this example, the `Index` action method retrieves data from the model, performs any necessary processing, and passes the data to the corresponding view for rendering.

1.5 Summary

Controllers play a crucial role in ASP.NET MVC as they handle user requests, coordinate the flow of data between the model and views, and determine the appropriate response to send back to the user. Controllers contain action methods that are invoked based on user requests, and they interact with the model to retrieve or manipulate data before passing it to the views.

Exercises:

1. Create a new controller in your ASP.NET MVC project.

2. Define action methods within the controller to handle specific user requests.

3. Test the controller by accessing the action methods through their corresponding URLs.

Chapter 2: Implementing Controller Actions

In this chapter, we will delve deeper into implementing controller actions in ASP.NET MVC. Controller actions are the methods within controllers that handle user requests and determine the appropriate response.

2.1 Anatomy of a Controller Action

A controller action is a public method within a controller class that is responsible for processing a specific user request. It performs the necessary operations, such as retrieving data from the model, performing business logic, and passing data to the view.

A controller action typically has the following components:

- Access Modifiers: Actions are typically defined as public methods to allow them to be accessible from other parts of the application.

- Method Signature: Actions may have parameters to receive data from the user, query strings, or form inputs.

- Return Type: Actions generally return an instance of the `ActionResult` class, which represents the result of the action.

2.2 Action Results

Action methods in ASP.NET MVC return an `ActionResult` or one of its derived types. These action results encapsulate the response to be sent back to the user.

Commonly used action results include:

- `ViewResult`: Represents the rendering of a view to be sent as the response.

- `RedirectResult`: Redirects the user to a different URL.

- `JsonResult`: Returns JSON data to the client.

- `PartialViewResult`: Renders a partial view to be sent as the response.

- `FileResult`: Sends a file to be downloaded by the user.

- `HttpNotFoundResult`: Returns a 404 "Not Found" error response.

2.3 Creating Controller Actions

To create a controller action in ASP.NET MVC, follow these steps:

1. Open the desired controller file.

2. Define a public method within the controller class, specifying the desired action name and any required parameters.

3. Implement the logic for the action method. Retrieve data from the model, perform business operations, and prepare the necessary data to be passed to the view.

4. Return an appropriate action result based on the desired response. For example:

```csharp
public ActionResult Index()
{
    var data = // retrieve data from the model or perform operations

    return View(data);
```

}

```
```

```csharp
public ActionResult Index()
{
    var data = // retrieve data from the model or perform operations

    return View(data);
}
```

In this example, the `Index` action retrieves data from the model and returns a `ViewResult`, passing the data to the corresponding view for rendering.

2.4 Handling HTTP Verbs

Controller actions can be decorated with attributes to specify the supported HTTP verbs (GET, POST, PUT, DELETE, etc.). By default, an action without a verb attribute is assumed to handle GET requests.

For example, to handle a POST request, decorate the action method with the `[HttpPost]` attribute:

```csharp
[HttpPost]

public ActionResult Create(FormData formData)

{
```

```
// Process the submitted form data


return RedirectToAction("Index");

}

```
```
[HttpPost]
public ActionResult Create(FormData formData)
{
    // Process the submitted form data

    return RedirectToAction("Index");
}
```

In this example, the `Create` action method is decorated with the `[HttpPost]` attribute, indicating that it should handle POST requests.

2.5 Summary

Controller actions are responsible for handling user requests, performing the necessary operations, and returning the appropriate response. They are defined as public methods within controllers and typically return an `ActionResult` or one of its derived types. Actions interact with the model, prepare data, and pass it to the views for rendering.

Exercises:

1. Implement additional controller actions in your ASP.NET MVC project to handle different user requests.

2. Return different types of action results based on the desired response.

3. Test the controller actions by accessing them through their corresponding URLs.

Chapter 3: Parameter Binding and Model Binding

In this chapter, we will explore parameter binding and model binding in ASP.NET MVC. Parameter binding allows you to receive data from user requests, while model binding simplifies the process of mapping incoming data to model objects.

3.1 Parameter Binding

Parameter binding in ASP.NET MVC enables you to receive data from user requests and use it within your controller actions. Parameters can be bound from various sources, such as route values, query strings, form inputs, or request headers.

To bind a parameter, you can include it as a parameter in your controller action method. The framework will automatically attempt to bind the parameter from the available sources based on its name and type.

Here's an example of parameter binding from a route value:

```csharp
public ActionResult Details(int id)
{
```

```
// Use the id parameter to retrieve data from the model


    return View();

}
```
```

```
public ActionResult Details(int id)
{
    // Use the id parameter to retrieve data from the model

    return View();
}
```

In this example, the `id` parameter is bound from a route value. The framework will attempt to match the value of `id` in the route to the parameter.

3.2 Model Binding

Model binding simplifies the process of mapping incoming data from user requests to model objects. It automatically maps form inputs, query string values, and other data to the properties of a model object, allowing you to work with the data in a structured manner.

To utilize model binding, you can include a model object as a parameter in your controller action method. The framework will
```

attempt to bind the incoming data to the properties of the model object.

Here's an example of model binding:

```csharp
[HttpPost]
public ActionResult Create(Product product)
{
    // Use the product object to save the submitted data to the model

    return RedirectToAction("Index");
}
```

```
[HttpPost]
public ActionResult Create(Product product)
{
    // Use the product object to save the submitted data to the model

    return RedirectToAction("Index");
}
```

In this example, the `Create` action method receives a `Product` object as a parameter. The framework will automatically bind the incoming form data to the properties of the `Product` object.

3.3 Model Binding Prefixes

Model binding prefixes are useful when you have multiple objects with similar property names in your view. By using a prefix, you can specify which object should be bound to which properties.

To use a model binding prefix, you can include it as a parameter in your action method:

```csharp
[HttpPost]

public ActionResult Edit(string prefix, Product product)

{

    // Use the prefix and product object to update the data in the model


    return RedirectToAction("Index");

}
```

```
[HttpPost]
public ActionResult Edit(string prefix, Product product)
{
    // Use the prefix and product object to update the data in the model

    return RedirectToAction("Index");
}
```

In this example, the `Edit` action method receives a prefix parameter that specifies the prefix to be used for model binding. This allows you to differentiate between properties of different objects with similar names.

3.4 Custom Model Binding

You can also create custom model binders in ASP.NET MVC to handle complex or non-standard binding scenarios. Custom model binders allow you to define custom logic for mapping the incoming data to your model objects.

To create a custom model binder, you need to implement the `IModelBinder` interface and register it with the framework.

3.5 Summary

Parameter binding and model binding are essential features in ASP.NET MVC that allow you to receive and work with data from user requests. Parameter binding enables you to bind data from various sources to your action method parameters, while model binding simplifies the mapping of incoming data to model objects. Custom model binders provide flexibility for handling complex or non-standard binding scenarios.

Exercises:

1. Create additional controller actions in your ASP.NET MVC project that utilize parameter binding.

2. Implement model binding in your controller actions to receive and work with data from user requests.

3. Test the parameter binding and model binding by passing data through the appropriate sources.

Chapter 4: Routing in ASP.NET MVC

Welcome to Day 4 of your journey to learn ASP.NET MVC! In this chapter, we will explore routing in ASP.NET MVC, which determines how URLs are mapped to controllers and actions. Routing plays a crucial role in defining the URL structure of your application and enabling user-friendly and search engine optimized URLs.

4.1 What is Routing?

Routing is the mechanism that maps incoming URLs to specific controller actions in ASP.NET MVC. It enables you to define custom URL patterns and configure how the application should handle different routes.

4.2 Default Routing Configuration

By default, ASP.NET MVC uses the following routing configuration:

```csharp
routes.MapRoute(
    name: "Default",
    url: "{controller}/{action}/{id}",
    defaults: new { controller = "Home", action = "Index", id = UrlParameter.Optional }
```

);

```
```

```
routes.MapRoute(
    name: "Default",
    url: "{controller}/{action}/{id}",
    defaults: new { controller = "Home", action = "Index", id = UrlParameter.Optional }
);
```

This default route configuration specifies that URLs should be in the format of `controller/action/id`, where `controller` and `action` correspond to the controller and action method names, respectively. The `id` parameter is optional and can be used to pass additional information.

For example, the URL `/Home/Index` would map to the `Index` action method within the `HomeController`.

4.3 Customizing Routes

You can customize routes to match your desired URL structure and provide user-friendly URLs. Custom routes can be added to the `RouteConfig.cs` file in the `App_Start` folder of your project.

To define a custom route, use the `MapRoute` method and specify the route URL pattern, controller, action, and any default values:

```csharp
```

```
routes.MapRoute(

    name: "CustomRoute",

    url: "custom/{id}",

    defaults: new { controller = "Home", action = "CustomAction", id =
UrlParameter.Optional }

);
```
```
routes.MapRoute(
    name: "CustomRoute",
    url: "custom/{id}",
    defaults: new { controller = "Home", action = "CustomAction", id = UrlParameter.Optional }
);
```

In this example, the route URL pattern is `custom/{id}`, which maps
to the `CustomAction` action method within the `HomeController`.
The `id` parameter is optional.

4.4 Route Constraints

Route constraints allow you to restrict the values that can be
matched by a particular route. Constraints are defined using regular
expressions and can be applied to route parameters.

For example, to restrict the `id` parameter in a route to be numeric,
you can use the following constraint:

````csharp
routes.MapRoute(

    name: "NumericId",

    url: "items/{id}",

    defaults: new { controller = "Items", action = "Details" },

    constraints: new { id = @"\d+" }

);
````

```
routes.MapRoute(
    name: "NumericId",
    url: "items/{id}",
    defaults: new { controller = "Items", action = "Details" },
    constraints: new { id = @"\d+" }
);
```

In this example, the route URL pattern is `items/{id}`, and the `id` parameter is restricted to numeric values using the constraint `@\d+`.

4.5 Attribute Routing

In addition to convention-based routing, ASP.NET MVC also supports attribute routing, which allows you to define routes directly on the controller and action method level using attributes.

To enable attribute routing, you need to add the following line of code in the `RouteConfig.cs` file:

```csharp
routes.MapMvcAttributeRoutes();
```

```
routes.MapMvcAttributeRoutes();
```

Once enabled, you can decorate your controllers and action methods with the `[Route]` attribute to specify custom routes:

```csharp
[Route("custom/{id}")]
public ActionResult CustomAction(int id)
{
    // Action logic here
}
```

```
[Route("custom/{id}")]
public ActionResult CustomAction(int id)
{
    // Action logic here
}
```

In this example, the `CustomAction` method is mapped to the URL `/custom/{id}` using the `[Route]` attribute.

4.6 Summary

Routing in ASP.NET MVC is responsible for mapping incoming URLs to specific controller actions. It enables you to define custom URL patterns, configure routes, and create user-friendly and search engine optimized URLs. Default routing is provided, and you can customize routes, apply constraints, and utilize attribute routing for more control over the URL structure of your application.

Exercises:

1. Customize the routes in your ASP.NET MVC project to match your desired URL structure.

2. Implement route constraints to restrict the values of route parameters.

3. Explore and utilize attribute routing in your controllers and action methods.

Chapter 5: Handling Errors and Exceptions

In this chapter, we will explore techniques for handling errors and exceptions in ASP.NET MVC. Error handling is an important aspect of building robust and user-friendly applications.

5.1 Understanding Error Handling in ASP.NET MVC

In ASP.NET MVC, error handling involves capturing and handling exceptions that occur during the processing of a user request. When an exception is thrown within a controller action or during the view rendering process, it needs to be caught and handled appropriately.

By default, ASP.NET MVC provides some built-in error handling mechanisms, but you can also customize error handling to suit your application's requirements.

5.2 Global Error Handling

Global error handling allows you to handle unhandled exceptions at the application level. By configuring global error handling, you can provide a centralized location to catch and process exceptions that occur anywhere within your application.

To implement global error handling, you can utilize the `Application_Error` event in the `Global.asax.cs` file. This event is raised when an unhandled exception occurs.

```csharp
protected void Application_Error(object sender, EventArgs e)
{
    // Log the error
    // Display a user-friendly error message
    // Redirect to an error page
}
```

```
protected void Application_Error(object sender, EventArgs e)
{
    // Log the error
    // Display a user-friendly error message
    // Redirect to an error page
}
```

In this event handler, you can log the error, display a user-friendly error message, and redirect the user to an error page.

5.3 Handling Errors within Controllers

Within controllers, you can handle errors by catching and processing exceptions within individual action methods. This allows you to handle specific exceptions in a more granular way and provide customized error responses.

To handle errors within a controller, you can use `try-catch` blocks to catch specific exceptions and perform appropriate error handling.

```csharp
public ActionResult Index()
{
    try
    {
        // Code that might throw an exception
    }
    catch (Exception ex)
    {
        // Log the error
        // Display a user-friendly error message
        // Return an appropriate action result (e.g., View, Redirect)
    }

    // Normal code execution
    // Return a normal action result
```

```
}

```

```
public ActionResult Index()
{
    try
    {
        // Code that might throw an exception
    }
    catch (Exception ex)
    {
        // Log the error
        // Display a user-friendly error message
        // Return an appropriate action result (e.g., View, Redirect)
    }

    // Normal code execution
    // Return a normal action result
}
```

In this example, the code within the `try` block is executed, and if an exception is thrown, it is caught in the `catch` block. You can log the error, display a user-friendly error message, and return an appropriate action result based on the error.

5.4 Custom Error Pages

Custom error pages allow you to display user-friendly error messages when an error occurs. You can create custom error pages for different HTTP status codes or for specific exceptions.

To configure custom error pages, you can use the `<customErrors>` element in the `Web.config` file:

```xml
<system.web>
  <customErrors mode="On" defaultRedirect="~/Error/Index">
    <error statusCode="404" redirect="~/Error/NotFound" />
    <error statusCode="500" redirect="~/Error/Internal" />
  </customErrors>
</system.web>
```

```
<system.web>
    <customErrors mode="On" defaultRedirect="~/Error/Index">
        <error statusCode="404" redirect="~/Error/NotFound" />
        <error statusCode="500" redirect="~/Error/Internal" />
    </customErrors>
</system.web>
```

In this example, custom error pages are configured for HTTP status codes 404 (Not Found) and 500 (Internal Server Error). When an error occurs, the user will be redirected to the corresponding custom error page.

5.5 Summary

Handling errors and exceptions is an important aspect of building robust applications in ASP.NET MVC. By implementing global error handling, handling errors within controllers, and configuring custom error pages, you can provide a better user experience and ensure that your application handles errors gracefully.

Exercises:

1. Implement global error handling in your ASP.NET MVC application to handle unhandled exceptions.

2. Handle specific errors within your controller action methods and provide appropriate error responses.

3. Configure custom error pages to display user-friendly error messages for different types of errors.

Day 5: Working with Data and Entity Framework

Welcome to Day 5 of your journey to learn ASP.NET MVC! In this chapter, we will focus on retrieving and displaying data in ASP.NET MVC using the Entity Framework. The Entity Framework is an ORM (Object-Relational Mapping) tool that simplifies database access and allows you to work with data as objects.

Chapter 1: Retrieving and Displaying Data

1.1 Setting up the Database Context

Before retrieving data, you need to set up the database context in your ASP.NET MVC project. The database context serves as a bridge between your application and the underlying database.

To set up the database context, follow these steps:

1. Create a class that derives from the `DbContext` class provided by the Entity Framework.

```csharp
public class ApplicationDbContext : DbContext
{
    // Define DbSet properties for your entities

    public DbSet<Product> Products { get; set; }

    // Additional DbSet properties for other entities
}
```

```csharp
public class ApplicationDbContext : DbContext
{
    // Define DbSet properties for your entities
    public DbSet<Product> Products { get; set; }
    // Additional DbSet properties for other entities
}
```

In this example, the `ApplicationDbContext` class derives from `DbContext` and defines a `DbSet` property for the `Product` entity.

2. In the `Web.config` file, add a connection string that specifies the connection details for your database.

```xml

<connectionStrings>

   <add name="DefaultConnection"
connectionString="your_connection_string"
providerName="System.Data.SqlClient" />

</connectionStrings>

```

```xml
<connectionStrings>
    <add name="DefaultConnection" connectionString="your_connection_string" providerName="System.Data
        .SqlClient" />
</connectionStrings>
```

Replace `"your_connection_string"` with the actual connection string for your database.

3. In the `Global.asax.cs` file, override the `Application_Start` method and initialize the database context.

```csharp
protected void Application_Start()
{
    // Other startup code

    Database.SetInitializer(new CreateDatabaseIfNotExists<ApplicationDbContext>());
    // Additional database initialization options

    // Other startup code
}
```

```
protected void Application_Start()
{
    // Other startup code

    Database.SetInitializer(new CreateDatabaseIfNotExists<ApplicationDbContext>());
    // Additional database initialization options

    // Other startup code
}
```

In this example, the `Application_Start` method initializes the database context using the `CreateDatabaseIfNotExists` initializer. You can choose different initialization options based on your requirements.

1.2 Retrieving Data from the Database

Once the database context is set up, you can retrieve data from the database using the Entity Framework.

To retrieve data, follow these steps:

1. Create an instance of the database context in your controller.

```csharp
private readonly ApplicationDbContext _context;

public HomeController()
{
    _context = new ApplicationDbContext();
}
```

```
private readonly ApplicationDbContext _context;

public HomeController()
{
    _context = new ApplicationDbContext();
}
```

In this example, the `ApplicationDbContext` is injected into the controller using dependency injection.

2. Query the database using LINQ (Language Integrated Query) to retrieve the desired data.

```csharp
public ActionResult Index()

{

    var products = _context.Products.ToList();

    return View(products);

}
```

```
public ActionResult Index()
{
    var products = _context.Products.ToList();
    return View(products);
}
```

In this example, the `Index` action method retrieves all the products from the database and passes them to the view for rendering.

3. Pass the retrieved data to the view for rendering.

```csharp

return View(products);

```

```
return View(products);
```

1.3 Displaying Data in Views

To display the retrieved data in a view, you can use the Razor view engine and HTML markup.

1. Create a view file that corresponds to the action method.

2. In the view file, iterate over the data and display it using HTML markup.

```html
@model List<Product>

@foreach (var product in Model)
{
    <div>
        <h3>@product.Name</h3>
        <p>@product.Description</p>
    </div>
}
```

```
@model List<Product>

@foreach (var product in Model)
{
    <div>
        <h3>@product.Name</h3>
        <p>@product.Description</p>
    </div>
}
```

In this example, the `@model` directive specifies the type of the model passed to the view. The `foreach` loop iterates over the products and displays their properties using Razor syntax.

1.4 Summary

Retrieving and displaying data is a fundamental aspect of building data-driven applications in ASP.NET MVC. By setting up the database context, querying the database using LINQ, and passing the retrieved data to the view, you can retrieve and display data from the database in your application.

Exercises:

1. Set up the database context in your ASP.NET MVC project.

2. Retrieve data from the database using the Entity Framework in one of your controller actions.

3. Display the retrieved data in a view using HTML markup and Razor syntax.

Chapter 2: Sorting and Filtering Data

In this chapter, we will focus on sorting and filtering data in ASP.NET MVC using the Entity Framework. Sorting and filtering are essential for providing a rich and interactive user experience when working with large datasets.

2.1 Sorting Data

Sorting data allows you to arrange the retrieved data in a specific order based on one or more columns. This enables users to view data in ascending or descending order, making it easier to find the desired information.

To implement sorting, follow these steps:

1. Modify your action method to accept a parameter for the sort order.

```csharp
public ActionResult Index(string sortOrder)

{

    // Code to retrieve data from the database


    // Apply sorting logic based on sortOrder parameter


    // Pass the sorted data to the view
```

```
    return View(sortedData);

}
```
```
public ActionResult Index(string sortOrder)
{
    // Code to retrieve data from the database

    // Apply sorting logic based on sortOrder parameter

    // Pass the sorted data to the view

    return View(sortedData);
}
```

2. Update the action method to apply sorting logic based on the `sortOrder` parameter.

```csharp
if (!string.IsNullOrEmpty(sortOrder))

{

    switch (sortOrder)

    {

        case "name_asc":

            sortedData = sortedData.OrderBy(p => p.Name);

            break;
```

```
case "name_desc":

    sortedData = sortedData.OrderByDescending(p => p.Name);

    break;

case "price_asc":

    sortedData = sortedData.OrderBy(p => p.Price);

    break;

case "price_desc":

    sortedData = sortedData.OrderByDescending(p => p.Price);

    break;

// Add more sorting options as needed

default:

    sortedData = sortedData.OrderBy(p => p.Name);

    break;

    }

}
```

```csharp
if (!string.IsNullOrEmpty(sortOrder))
{
    switch (sortOrder)
    {
        case "name_asc":
            sortedData = sortedData.OrderBy(p => p.Name);
            break;
        case "name_desc":
            sortedData = sortedData.OrderByDescending(p => p.Name);
            break;
        case "price_asc":
            sortedData = sortedData.OrderBy(p => p.Price);
            break;
        case "price_desc":
            sortedData = sortedData.OrderByDescending(p => p.Price);
            break;
        // Add more sorting options as needed
        default:
            sortedData = sortedData.OrderBy(p => p.Name);
            break;
    }
}
```

In this example, the `sortOrder` parameter is used to determine the sorting logic. The data is sorted based on the selected sorting option.

3. Pass the sorted data to the view for rendering.

```csharp
return View(sortedData);
```

```csharp
return View(sortedData);
```

2.2 Filtering Data

Filtering data allows users to narrow down the displayed data based on specific criteria or search terms. Filtering helps users find the information they need quickly and efficiently.

To implement filtering, follow these steps:

1. Modify your action method to accept a parameter for the filter criteria.

```csharp
public ActionResult Index(string searchCriteria)
{
    // Code to retrieve data from the database

    // Apply filtering logic based on searchCriteria parameter

    // Pass the filtered data to the view

    return View(filteredData);
}
```

```csharp
public ActionResult Index(string searchCriteria)
{
    // Code to retrieve data from the database

    // Apply filtering logic based on searchCriteria parameter

    // Pass the filtered data to the view

    return View(filteredData);
}
```

2. Update the action method to apply filtering logic based on the `searchCriteria` parameter.

```csharp

if (!string.IsNullOrEmpty(searchCriteria))

{

    filteredData = filteredData.Where(p =>
p.Name.Contains(searchCriteria));

}

```

```csharp
if (!string.IsNullOrEmpty(searchCriteria))
{
    filteredData = filteredData.Where(p => p.Name.Contains(searchCriteria));
}
```

In this example, the `searchCriteria` parameter is used to filter the data based on the product name. Only the products containing the search criteria in their names will be included in the filtered data.

3. Pass the filtered data to the view for rendering.

```csharp
return View(filteredData);
```

```
return View(filteredData);
```

2.3 Summary

Sorting and filtering data are important features in ASP.NET MVC that enhance the user experience and make it easier to navigate and find information within large datasets. By implementing sorting logic based on user-selected options and applying filtering logic based on search criteria, you can provide users with powerful data manipulation capabilities.

Exercises:

1. Modify one of your action methods to implement sorting functionality based on user-selected options.

2. Update another action method to include filtering functionality based on user-provided search criteria.

3. Test the sorting and filtering features by interacting with the corresponding views.

Chapter 3: Implementing Paging and Pagination

In this chapter, we will focus on implementing paging and pagination in ASP.NET MVC using the Entity Framework. Paging allows you to divide large datasets into smaller, manageable chunks, while pagination provides navigation controls to browse through the data.

3.1 Understanding Paging and Pagination

Paging refers to the process of dividing a large dataset into smaller subsets, or pages, to improve performance and reduce the amount of data displayed at once. Pagination, on the other hand, provides user interface controls to navigate through the different pages of data.

By implementing paging and pagination, you can enhance the user experience and make it easier for users to navigate through large datasets.

3.2 Implementing Paging

To implement paging in ASP.NET MVC, follow these steps:

1. Modify your action method to accept parameters for the page number and page size.

```csharp
public ActionResult Index(int? page, int pageSize = 10)
{
    // Code to retrieve data from the database

    // Apply paging logic based on page and pageSize parameters

    // Pass the paged data to the view

    return View(pagedData);
}
```

```csharp
public ActionResult Index(int? page, int pageSize = 10)
{
    // Code to retrieve data from the database

    // Apply paging logic based on page and pageSize parameters

    // Pass the paged data to the view

    return View(pagedData);
}
```

2. Update the action method to apply paging logic based on the `page` and `pageSize` parameters.

```csharp
int pageNumber = (page ?? 1);

pagedData = data.Skip((pageNumber - 1) * pageSize).Take(pageSize);
```

```csharp
int pageNumber = (page ?? 1);
pagedData = data.Skip((pageNumber - 1) * pageSize).Take(pageSize);
```

In this example, the `page` parameter determines the current page number, and the `pageSize` parameter specifies the number of items to display per page. The data is then filtered based on the current page number and page size.

3. Pass the paged data to the view for rendering.

```csharp
return View(pagedData);
```

```csharp
return View(pagedData);
```

3.3 Implementing Pagination

To implement pagination in ASP.NET MVC, you can utilize HTML markup and Razor syntax to generate navigation controls.

1. Determine the total number of pages based on the total number of items and the page size.

```csharp
int totalItems = data.Count();
int totalPages = (int)Math.Ceiling((double)totalItems / pageSize);
```

```
int totalItems = data.Count();
int totalPages = (int)Math.Ceiling((double)totalItems / pageSize);
```

In this example, the `totalItems` variable represents the total number of items, and the `totalPages` variable calculates the total number of pages based on the page size.

2. Generate navigation controls in your view to allow users to navigate through the pages.

```html
@for (int i = 1; i <= totalPages; i++)
{
    <a href="@Url.Action("Index", new { page = i })">@i</a>
```

```
}
```

```
```

```
@for (int i = 1; i <= totalPages; i++)
{
    <a href="@Url.Action("Index", new { page = i })">@i</a>
}
```

In this example, a loop generates navigation links for each page. The `Url.Action` method is used to generate the URL for each page, passing the current page number as a parameter.

3.4 Summary

Implementing paging and pagination in ASP.NET MVC allows you to divide large datasets into smaller, manageable chunks and provide navigation controls for users to browse through the data. By accepting parameters for the page number and page size, applying paging logic, and generating pagination controls in your views, you can enhance the user experience and improve the performance of your application when working with large datasets.

Exercises:

1. Modify one of your action methods to implement paging functionality based on the current page number and page size.

2. Generate pagination controls in the corresponding view to allow users to navigate through the pages.

3. Test the paging and pagination features by interacting with the views and navigating through the data.

Chapter 4: Updating and Deleting Data

In this chapter, we will focus on updating and deleting data in ASP.NET MVC using the Entity Framework. Updating and deleting data are important operations when working with persistent data in an application.

4.1 Updating Data

To update data in ASP.NET MVC, follow these steps:

1. Retrieve the data to be updated from the database.

```csharp
public ActionResult Edit(int id)
{
    var product = _context.Products.Find(id);

    return View(product);
}
```

```
public ActionResult Edit(int id)
{
    var product = _context.Products.Find(id);
    return View(product);
}
```

In this example, the `Edit` action method retrieves the product with the specified `id` from the database.

2. Display the data in a view to allow the user to modify it.

```html
@model Product

@using (Html.BeginForm())

{

  <div>

    @Html.LabelFor(model => model.Name)

    @Html.TextBoxFor(model => model.Name)

  </div>


  <div>

    @Html.LabelFor(model => model.Price)

    @Html.TextBoxFor(model => model.Price)
```

```
</div>

<input type="submit" value="Update" />

}
```

```
@model Product

@using (Html.BeginForm())
{
    <div>
        @Html.LabelFor(model => model.Name)
        @Html.TextBoxFor(model => model.Name)
    </div>

    <div>
        @Html.LabelFor(model => model.Price)
        @Html.TextBoxFor(model => model.Price)
    </div>

    <input type="submit" value="Update" />
}
```

In this example, the `TextBoxFor` helper method generates input fields for the `Name` and `Price` properties of the `Product` model.

3. Handle the form submission in a post action method and update the data in the database.

```csharp
```

```
[HttpPost]

public ActionResult Edit(Product product)

{

  if (ModelState.IsValid)

  {

    _context.Entry(product).State = EntityState.Modified;

    _context.SaveChanges();

    return RedirectToAction("Index");

  }

  return View(product);

}
```

```
[HttpPost]
public ActionResult Edit(Product product)
{
    if (ModelState.IsValid)
    {
        _context.Entry(product).State = EntityState.Modified;
        _context.SaveChanges();
        return RedirectToAction("Index");
    }

    return View(product);
}
```

In this example, the `Edit` action method is decorated with the
`[HttpPost]` attribute to handle the form submission. The modified

`Product` object is attached to the context, and the changes are saved to the database.

4.2 Deleting Data

To delete data in ASP.NET MVC, follow these steps:

1. Retrieve the data to be deleted from the database.

```csharp
public ActionResult Delete(int id)

{

    var product = _context.Products.Find(id);

    return View(product);

}
```

```csharp
public ActionResult Delete(int id)
{
    var product = _context.Products.Find(id);
    return View(product);
}
```

In this example, the `Delete` action method retrieves the product with the specified `id` from the database.

2. Display the data in a view to confirm the deletion.

```html
@model Product


<h3>Are you sure you want to delete this product?</h3>


<p>Name: @Model.Name</p>

<p>Price: @Model.Price</p>

@using (Html.BeginForm())

{

    <input type="submit" value="Delete" />

}
```

```
@model Product

<h3>Are you sure you want to delete this product?</h3>

<p>Name: @Model.Name</p>
<p>Price: @Model.Price</p>

@using (Html.BeginForm())
{
    <input type="submit" value="Delete" />
}
```

In this example, the product details are displayed, and a confirmation form is provided.

3. Handle the form submission in a post action method and delete the data from the database.

```csharp
[HttpPost, ActionName("Delete")]

public ActionResult DeleteConfirmed(int id)

{

    var product = _context.Products.Find(id);

    _context.Products.Remove(product);

    _context.SaveChanges();

    return RedirectToAction("Index");

}
```

```csharp
[HttpPost, ActionName("Delete")]
public ActionResult DeleteConfirmed(int id)
{
    var product = _context.Products.Find(id);
    _context.Products.Remove(product);
    _context.SaveChanges();
    return RedirectToAction("Index");
}
```

In this example, the `DeleteConfirmed` action method is decorated with the `[HttpPost]` and `ActionName` attributes to handle the form submission. The specified product is removed from the context and deleted from the database.

4.3 Summary

Updating and deleting data are important operations when working with persistent data in ASP.NET MVC. By retrieving the data to be updated or deleted, displaying it in views, handling form submissions, and applying the necessary changes to the database using the Entity Framework, you can effectively manage the data in your application.

Exercises:

1. Implement the update functionality in one of your ASP.NET MVC actions to allow users to modify data.

2. Add the delete functionality to another action, enabling users to delete data from the database.

3. Test the update and delete features by interacting with the corresponding views and verifying the changes in the database.

Chapter 5: Implementing Advanced Querying Techniques

In this chapter, we will explore advanced querying techniques in ASP.NET MVC using the Entity Framework. Advanced querying techniques allow you to perform complex queries and retrieve specific subsets of data from the database.

5.1 Filtering Data with Multiple Conditions

When filtering data, you may need to apply multiple conditions to retrieve a specific subset of data. The Entity Framework provides various methods and operators to combine conditions in a query.

To filter data with multiple conditions, follow these steps:

1. Define the conditions using LINQ expressions.

```csharp
public ActionResult Index()
{
    var filteredData = _context.Products.Where(p => p.Category == "Electronics" && p.Price > 500);

    return View(filteredData);
}
```

```
public ActionResult Index()
{
    var filteredData = _context.Products.Where(p => p.Category == "Electronics" && p.Price > 500);
    return View(filteredData);
}
```

In this example, the `Where` method is used to define the conditions for filtering the products. Only products with the category "Electronics" and a price greater than 500 will be included in the filtered data.

2. Pass the filtered data to the view for rendering.

```csharp

return View(filteredData);

```

```
return View(filteredData);
```

5.2 Sorting Data with Multiple Columns

In some cases, you may need to sort data based on multiple columns. The Entity Framework allows you to specify multiple sorting criteria in a query.

To sort data with multiple columns, follow these steps:

1. Use the `OrderBy` and `ThenBy` methods to specify the sorting criteria.

```csharp
public ActionResult Index()
{
    var sortedData = _context.Products.OrderBy(p =>
p.Category).ThenBy(p => p.Price);

    return View(sortedData);
}
```

```csharp
public ActionResult Index()
{
    var sortedData = _context.Products.OrderBy(p => p.Category).ThenBy(p => p.Price);
    return View(sortedData);
}
```

In this example, the `OrderBy` method is used to sort the products by category in ascending order, and the `ThenBy` method is used to sort the products with the same category by price in ascending order.

2. Pass the sorted data to the view for rendering.

```csharp
return View(sortedData);
```

```
return View(sortedData);
```

5.3 Performing Aggregations and Calculations

The Entity Framework provides built-in methods for performing aggregations and calculations on data. These methods allow you to retrieve summarized information from the database.

To perform aggregations and calculations, follow these steps:

1. Use the appropriate aggregation or calculation methods provided by the Entity Framework.

```csharp
public ActionResult Index()
{
    var totalProducts = _context.Products.Count();

    var averagePrice = _context.Products.Average(p => p.Price);

    var totalPrice = _context.Products.Sum(p => p.Price);

    // Pass the calculated values to the view

    return View();
}
```

```
public ActionResult Index()
{
    var totalProducts = _context.Products.Count();
    var averagePrice = _context.Products.Average(p => p.Price);
    var totalPrice = _context.Products.Sum(p => p.Price);

    // Pass the calculated values to the view

    return View();
}
```

In this example, the `Count` method is used to retrieve the total number of products, the `Average` method is used to calculate the average price of the products, and the `Sum` method is used to calculate the total price of the products.

2. Pass the calculated values to the view for rendering.

```csharp

ViewBag.TotalProducts = totalProducts;

ViewBag.AveragePrice = averagePrice;

ViewBag.TotalPrice = totalPrice;


return View();
```

```
ViewBag.TotalProducts = totalProducts;
ViewBag.AveragePrice = averagePrice;
ViewBag.TotalPrice = totalPrice;

return View();
```

3. Display the calculated values in the view using Razor syntax.

```html
<p>Total Products: @ViewBag.TotalProducts</p>

<p>Average Price: @ViewBag.AveragePrice</p>

<p>Total Price: @ViewBag.TotalPrice</p>
```

```
<p>Total Products: @ViewBag.TotalProducts</p>
<p>Average Price: @ViewBag.AveragePrice</p>
<p>Total Price: @ViewBag.TotalPrice</p>
```

5.4 Limiting the Number of Results

In some scenarios, you may want to retrieve only a specific number of results from the database. The Entity Framework provides the `Take` method to limit the number of results in a query.

To limit the number of results, follow these steps:

1. Use the `Take` method to specify the maximum number of results to retrieve.

```csharp
public ActionResult Index()
```

```
{

    var limitedData = _context.Products.Take(10);

    return View(limitedData);

}
```
```
public ActionResult Index()
{
    var limitedData = _context.Products.Take(10);
    return View(limitedData);
}
```

In this example, the `Take` method is used to retrieve only the first 10 products from the database.

2. Pass the limited data to the view for rendering.

```csharp
return View(limitedData);
```
```
return View(limitedData);
```

5.5 Summary

Implementing advanced querying techniques in ASP.NET MVC allows you to perform complex queries and retrieve specific subsets of data from the database. By filtering data with multiple conditions, sorting data with multiple columns, performing aggregations and calculations, and limiting the number of results, you can retrieve and manipulate data in a flexible and efficient manner.

Exercises:

1. Modify one of your action methods to implement filtering with multiple conditions based on user-selected options.

2. Update another action method to implement sorting with multiple columns based on user-selected options.

3. Implement an aggregation or calculation in a different action method to retrieve summarized information from the database.

4. Test the advanced querying techniques by interacting with the corresponding views and verifying the retrieved data.

Great job completing Day 5!

Day 6: Authentication and Authorization

Welcome to Day 6 of your journey to learn ASP.NET MVC! In this chapter, we will explore authentication and authorization, two important concepts in web application security. Authentication verifies the identity of users, while authorization determines the actions they are allowed to perform.

Chapter 1: Introduction to Authentication and Authorization

1.1 What is Authentication?

Authentication is the process of verifying the identity of users accessing a web application. It ensures that only authorized individuals can access protected resources and perform certain actions.

In ASP.NET MVC, authentication can be implemented using various techniques, such as forms authentication, Windows authentication, or external authentication providers (e.g., OAuth).

1.2 What is Authorization?

Authorization is the process of granting or denying access to specific resources or actions within a web application. It ensures that authenticated users have the necessary permissions to perform certain operations.

In ASP.NET MVC, authorization is typically implemented using roles and claims. Roles define sets of users with common access rights, while claims represent specific permissions associated with users.

1.3 Forms Authentication in ASP.NET MVC

Forms authentication is a common authentication method in ASP.NET MVC. It involves verifying user credentials against a user store (e.g., a database), issuing authentication tokens (usually in the form of cookies), and validating those tokens on subsequent requests.

To implement forms authentication in ASP.NET MVC, you need to configure authentication settings in the `Web.config` file, define a user store (e.g., a database table), and use the `Authorize` attribute to restrict access to controllers or actions.

1.4 Role-Based Authorization in ASP.NET MVC

Role-based authorization allows you to control access to specific resources based on predefined roles. Users are assigned to roles, and permissions are associated with those roles.

To implement role-based authorization in ASP.NET MVC, you need to define roles, associate users with roles, and use the `Authorize` attribute with role names or roles defined in the `Web.config` file.

1.5 Claims-Based Authorization in ASP.NET MVC

Claims-based authorization allows you to control access to specific resources based on fine-grained permissions. Claims represent specific pieces of information about a user, such as their role, email address, or custom attributes.

To implement claims-based authorization in ASP.NET MVC, you need to define claims, associate claims with users, and use the `Authorize` attribute with specific claim types or values.

1.6 Summary

Authentication and authorization are crucial aspects of web application security. Authentication verifies the identity of users, while authorization controls their access to resources and actions. In ASP.NET MVC, you can implement authentication using various techniques, such as forms authentication, and control authorization using roles or claims.

Exercises:

1. Research and choose an authentication method suitable for your ASP.NET MVC project.

2. Identify the resources or actions that require authorization in your application.

3. Implement role-based authorization for a specific controller or action.

Chapter 2: Implementing User Registration and Login

In this chapter, we will focus on implementing user registration and login functionality in ASP.NET MVC. User registration allows new users to create accounts, while login enables existing users to authenticate and access protected resources.

2.1 User Registration

User registration involves collecting user information and creating user accounts in the system. In ASP.NET MVC, user registration can be implemented using forms and interacting with a user store, such as a database.

To implement user registration, follow these steps:

1. Create a registration view to collect user information, such as username, password, email, etc.

```html
@model RegistrationViewModel

@using (Html.BeginForm())
```

```
{
    <div>
        @Html.LabelFor(model => model.Username)
        @Html.TextBoxFor(model => model.Username)
    </div>

    <div>
        @Html.LabelFor(model => model.Password)
        @Html.PasswordFor(model => model.Password)
    </div>

    <!-- Add more input fields for other user information -->

    <input type="submit" value="Register" />
}
```
```
```

```
@model RegistrationViewModel

@using (Html.BeginForm())
{
    <div>
        @Html.LabelFor(model => model.Username)
        @Html.TextBoxFor(model => model.Username)
    </div>

    <div>
        @Html.LabelFor(model => model.Password)
        @Html.PasswordFor(model => model.Password)
    </div>

    <!-- Add more input fields for other user information -->

    <input type="submit" value="Register" />
}
```

In this example, the `RegistrationViewModel` represents the user information to be collected. The `Html` helper methods generate input fields for the properties of the view model.

2. Create a registration action method to handle the form submission.

```csharp

[HttpPost]

public ActionResult Register(RegistrationViewModel model)
```

```
{
    if (ModelState.IsValid)
    {
        // Create a new user and save it in the user store (e.g., database)

        // Redirect to a success page or login page
    }

    return View(model);
}
```

```
[HttpPost]
public ActionResult Register(RegistrationViewModel model)
{
    if (ModelState.IsValid)
    {
        // Create a new user and save it in the user store (e.g., database)

        // Redirect to a success page or login page
    }

    return View(model);
}
```

In this example, the `Register` action method is decorated with the `[HttpPost]` attribute to handle the form submission. The

`ModelState.IsValid` property is used to validate the user input. If the input is valid, a new user account can be created and saved in the user store.

2.2 User Login

User login allows authenticated users to access protected resources by verifying their credentials. In ASP.NET MVC, user login can be implemented using forms authentication and validating the user credentials against the user store.

To implement user login, follow these steps:

1. Create a login view to collect user credentials, such as username and password.

```html
@using (Html.BeginForm())
{
  <div>

    @Html.LabelFor(model => model.Username)

    @Html.TextBoxFor(model => model.Username)

  </div>
```

```
    <div>

        @Html.LabelFor(model => model.Password)

        @Html.PasswordFor(model => model.Password)

    </div>


    <input type="submit" value="Login" />

}
```
```
@using (Html.BeginForm())
{
    <div>
        @Html.LabelFor(model => model.Username)
        @Html.TextBoxFor(model => model.Username)
    </div>

    <div>
        @Html.LabelFor(model => model.Password)
        @Html.PasswordFor(model => model.Password)
    </div>

    <input type="submit" value="Login" />
}
```

In this example, the input fields are generated using the `Html` helper methods for the `Username` and `Password` properties of the login view model.

2. Create a login action method to handle the form submission.

```csharp
[HttpPost]
public ActionResult Login(LoginViewModel model)
{
    if (ModelState.IsValid)
    {
        // Validate the user credentials against the user store

        // Set authentication cookies or tokens

        // Redirect to the home page or a protected resource
    }

    return View(model);
}
```

```
[HttpPost]
public ActionResult Login(LoginViewModel model)
{
    if (ModelState.IsValid)
    {
        // Validate the user credentials against the user store

        // Set authentication cookies or tokens

        // Redirect to the home page or a protected resource
    }

    return View(model);
}
```

In this example, the `Login` action method is decorated with the `[HttpPost]` attribute to handle the form submission. The `ModelState.IsValid` property is used to validate the user input. If the input is valid, the user credentials can be validated against the user store, and authentication cookies or tokens can be set.

2.3 Summary

Implementing user registration and login functionality is essential for providing secure access to web applications. By collecting user information, creating user accounts, validating user input, and managing authentication tokens or cookies, you can enable users to register and login to your ASP.NET MVC application.

Exercises:

1. Implement user registration functionality in your ASP.NET MVC application.

2. Add user login functionality to your application using forms authentication.

3. Test the registration and login features by interacting with the corresponding views and verifying user accounts.

Chapter 3: Securing Controllers and Actions

In this chapter, we will focus on securing controllers and actions in ASP.NET MVC by applying authorization rules. Securing controllers and actions ensures that only authorized users can access protected resources and perform certain actions.

3.1 Applying Authorization to Controllers

To apply authorization to controllers in ASP.NET MVC, you can use the `[Authorize]` attribute. The `[Authorize]` attribute allows you to specify which users or roles have access to the controller and its actions.

To apply the `[Authorize]` attribute to a controller, follow these steps:

1. Decorate the controller class with the `[Authorize]` attribute.

```csharp
[Authorize]

public class AdminController : Controller

{

    // Controller code
```

}

```

```

```
[Authorize]
public class AdminController : Controller
{
    // Controller code
}
```

In this example, the `[Authorize]` attribute is applied to the `AdminController` class, indicating that only authenticated users can access the controller and its actions.

2. Optionally, you can specify roles or users allowed to access the controller.

```csharp

[Authorize(Roles = "Admin")]

public class AdminController : Controller

{

    // Controller code

}

```

```
[Authorize(Roles = "Admin")]
public class AdminController : Controller
{
    // Controller code
}
```

In this example, the `[Authorize(Roles = "Admin")]` attribute restricts access to the `AdminController` to users assigned the "Admin" role.

3.2 Applying Authorization to Actions

In addition to securing controllers, you can apply authorization rules to individual actions within a controller. This allows you to further fine-tune access control based on specific actions.

To apply authorization to an action, follow these steps:

1. Decorate the action method with the `[Authorize]` attribute.

```csharp
public class AdminController : Controller
{
    [Authorize]
    public ActionResult Dashboard()
    {
```

```
    // Action code

  }

}
```
```

```csharp
public class AdminController : Controller
{
    [Authorize]
    public ActionResult Dashboard()
    {
        // Action code
    }
}
```

In this example, the `[Authorize]` attribute is applied to the
`Dashboard` action method, indicating that only authenticated users
can access this action.

2. Optionally, you can specify roles or users allowed to access the
action.

```csharp

public class AdminController : Controller

{

  [Authorize(Roles = "Admin")]

  public ActionResult Dashboard()
```
```

```
{
    // Action code
}
}
```

```
public class AdminController : Controller
{
    [Authorize(Roles = "Admin")]
    public ActionResult Dashboard()
    {
        // Action code
    }
}
```

In this example, the `[Authorize(Roles = "Admin")]` attribute restricts access to the `Dashboard` action to users assigned the "Admin" role.

3.3 Handling Unauthorized Access

When an unauthorized user attempts to access a secured controller or action, ASP.NET MVC redirects them to the login page by default. You can customize this behavior by configuring the authentication settings in the `Web.config` file or by handling unauthorized access programmatically.

To customize the behavior for unauthorized access, you can:

- Set a specific redirect URL:

```csharp
<system.web>

  <authentication mode="Forms">

    <forms loginUrl="~/Account/Login" />

  </authentication>

</system.web>
```

```
<system.web>
  <authentication mode="Forms">
    <forms loginUrl="~/Account/Login" />
  </authentication>
</system.web>
```

- Handle unauthorized access programmatically:

```csharp
protected override void
HandleUnauthorizedRequest(AuthorizationContext filterContext)

{

    // Custom logic to handle unauthorized access

    filterContext.Result = new RedirectResult("~/Account/Login");

}
```

```
protected override void HandleUnauthorizedRequest(AuthorizationContext filterContext)
{
    // Custom logic to handle unauthorized access
    filterContext.Result = new RedirectResult("~/Account/Login");
}
```

3.4 Summary

Securing controllers and actions in ASP.NET MVC is crucial to ensure that only authorized users can access protected resources and perform specific actions. By applying the `[Authorize]` attribute to controllers or actions and specifying the required roles or users, you can control access to various parts of your application. Additionally, you can customize the behavior for unauthorized access to provide a seamless and secure user experience.

Exercises:

1. Apply the `[Authorize]` attribute to specific controllers or actions in your ASP.NET MVC application.

2. Test the access control by logging in with different user accounts and verifying the allowed or denied access to protected resources.

Chapter 4: Implementing Role-Based Authorization

In this chapter, we will focus on implementing role-based authorization in ASP.NET MVC. Role-based authorization allows you to control access to specific resources based on predefined roles. Users are assigned to roles, and permissions are associated with those roles.

4.1 Defining Roles

Before implementing role-based authorization, you need to define roles that will be used to control access to resources in your application. Roles can be defined in various ways, such as using a database table or a configuration file.

To define roles, follow these steps:

1. Create a roles table in your database or a configuration file to store the roles.

2. Add the necessary roles to the roles table or configuration file. For example, you can have roles like "Admin," "User," or "Manager" based on the requirements of your application.

3. Optionally, create a mapping between users and roles. This can be stored in a separate table or as a property of the user entity.

4.2 Applying Role-Based Authorization

To apply role-based authorization to controllers and actions in ASP.NET MVC, you can use the `[Authorize(Roles = "RoleName")]` attribute. The `[Authorize(Roles = "RoleName")]` attribute allows you to specify which roles have access to the controller or action.

To apply role-based authorization, follow these steps:

1. Decorate the controller or action with the `[Authorize(Roles = "RoleName")]` attribute.

```csharp
[Authorize(Roles = "Admin")]

public class AdminController : Controller

{

    // Controller code

}
```

```csharp
[Authorize(Roles = "Admin")]
public class AdminController : Controller
{
    // Controller code
}
```

In this example, only users assigned the "Admin" role can access the `AdminController` and its actions.

2. Optionally, you can apply multiple roles to the `[Authorize]` attribute.

```csharp

[Authorize(Roles = "Admin, Manager")]

public class AdminController : Controller

{

  // Controller code

}

```

```csharp
[Authorize(Roles = "Admin, Manager")]
public class AdminController : Controller
{
    // Controller code
}
```

In this example, users assigned either the "Admin" or "Manager" role can access the `AdminController` and its actions.

4.3 Dynamic Role-Based Authorization

In some cases, you may need to perform dynamic role-based authorization based on specific conditions or business rules. You can achieve this by implementing a custom authorization filter.

To implement dynamic role-based authorization, follow these steps:

1. Create a custom authorization filter by implementing the `IAuthorizationFilter` interface.

```csharp
public class CustomAuthorizationFilter : IAuthorizationFilter

{

    public void OnAuthorization(AuthorizationContext filterContext)

    {

        // Implement your custom authorization logic based on
conditions or business rules

    }

}
```

```
public class CustomAuthorizationFilter : IAuthorizationFilter
{
    public void OnAuthorization(AuthorizationContext filterContext)
    {
        // Implement your custom authorization logic based on conditions or business rules
    }
}
```

2. Register the custom authorization filter globally or apply it selectively to controllers or actions using the `[CustomAuthorizationFilter]` attribute.

```csharp
[CustomAuthorizationFilter]
public class MyController : Controller
{
    // Controller code
}
```

```
[CustomAuthorizationFilter]
public class MyController : Controller
{
    // Controller code
}
```

In this example, the `CustomAuthorizationFilter` will be invoked for every request to the `MyController` and can perform dynamic role-based authorization based on specific conditions.

4.4 Summary

Implementing role-based authorization in ASP.NET MVC allows you to control access to specific resources based on predefined roles. By applying the `[Authorize(Roles = "RoleName")]` attribute to controllers or actions and specifying the required roles, you can restrict access to certain parts of your application. Additionally, you can implement custom authorization filters to perform dynamic role-based authorization based on specific conditions or business rules.

Exercises:

1. Define roles for your ASP.NET MVC application based on the required access levels.

2. Apply role-based authorization to specific controllers or actions using the `[Authorize(Roles = "RoleName")]` attribute.

3. Test the access control by logging in with different user accounts assigned different roles and verifying the allowed or denied access to protected resources.

Chapter 5: Customizing Authentication and Authorization

In this chapter, we will focus on customizing authentication and authorization in ASP.NET MVC. Customization allows you to tailor the authentication and authorization process to meet the specific requirements of your application.

5.1 Customizing Authentication

Authentication customization involves modifying the default authentication settings and behavior in ASP.NET MVC. Some common customization options include:

1. Configuring authentication settings in the `Web.config` file:

   - You can specify authentication modes, default login pages, cookie settings, etc.

2. Implementing custom authentication providers:

   - You can integrate external authentication providers, such as OAuth or OpenID, for user authentication.

3. Using custom authentication filters:

- You can implement custom authorization filters or authentication filters to add additional authentication logic or perform custom authentication checks.

By customizing authentication, you can extend the default functionality of ASP.NET MVC and tailor it to fit your specific authentication requirements.

5.2 Customizing Authorization

Authorization customization involves implementing custom authorization logic in ASP.NET MVC. Some common customization options include:

1. Implementing custom authorization filters:

   - You can create custom authorization filters by implementing the `IAuthorizationFilter` interface. These filters can perform additional authorization checks based on specific conditions or business rules.

2. Adding custom authorization attributes:

   - You can create custom authorization attributes by inheriting from the `AuthorizeAttribute` class. These attributes can encapsulate complex authorization rules and simplify the application of authorization to controllers and actions.

3. Using custom authorization policies:

  - You can define custom authorization policies using the policy-based authorization system in ASP.NET MVC. These policies allow you to express complex authorization rules and apply them to controllers and actions.

By customizing authorization, you can implement fine-grained access control and enforce specific authorization rules that go beyond the built-in functionality of ASP.NET MVC.

5.3 Summary

Customizing authentication and authorization in ASP.NET MVC allows you to tailor the authentication and authorization process to meet the specific requirements of your application. By modifying authentication settings, implementing custom authentication providers, using custom authentication filters, implementing custom authorization filters or attributes, and using custom authorization policies, you can extend and enhance the default functionality of ASP.NET MVC to provide a secure and customized authentication and authorization experience.

Exercises:

1. Research and implement a custom authentication provider in your ASP.NET MVC application.

2. Create a custom authorization filter or attribute to perform additional authorization checks based on specific conditions.

3. Test the custom authentication and authorization features by interacting with the corresponding views and verifying the authentication and authorization results.

Day 7: Advanced Topics and Best Practices

Welcome to Day 7 of your journey to learn ASP.NET MVC! In this chapter, we will explore the topic of caching and how it can be implemented in ASP.NET MVC to improve performance. Caching allows you to store frequently accessed data or rendered content in memory, reducing the need for repetitive computations and database queries.

Chapter 1: Implementing Caching for Performance Optimization

1.1 Understanding Caching in ASP.NET MVC

Caching is the process of storing data or content in memory for quick retrieval. In ASP.NET MVC, caching can be applied at different levels, including server-side caching, client-side caching, and output caching.

- Server-side caching: This involves caching data or content on the server-side, reducing the need for repetitive computations or expensive operations.

- Client-side caching: This involves caching data or content on the client-side, allowing the client to reuse the cached resources without making additional requests to the server.

- Output caching: This involves caching the output of an entire action or view, storing the rendered content in memory and serving it directly to subsequent requests.

1.2 Implementing Server-side Caching

To implement server-side caching in ASP.NET MVC, you can utilize the `MemoryCache` class or other caching mechanisms provided by the .NET framework. Server-side caching can be used to cache data retrieved from a database, computed values, or any other frequently accessed data.

To implement server-side caching, follow these steps:

1. Create an instance of the `MemoryCache` class or use the caching mechanism provided by your preferred caching library.

2. Store the data or content in the cache with a unique key and an optional expiration time.

```csharp
MemoryCache cache = MemoryCache.Default;

var cachedData = cache.Get("CacheKey");


if (cachedData == null)

{

    // Data not found in cache, retrieve it from the source and store it in the cache

    cachedData = GetDataFromSource();

    cache.Set("CacheKey", cachedData, TimeSpan.FromMinutes(30)); // Cache for 30 minutes
```

}

// Use the cachedData for further processing

```

```

```csharp
MemoryCache cache = MemoryCache.Default;
var cachedData = cache.Get("CacheKey");

if (cachedData == null)
{
    // Data not found in cache, retrieve it from the source and store it in the cache
    cachedData = GetDataFromSource();
    cache.Set("CacheKey", cachedData, TimeSpan.FromMinutes(30)); // Cache for 30 minutes
}

// Use the cachedData for further processing
```

In this example, the `MemoryCache` class is used to store and retrieve data. The `Get` method is used to check if the data exists in the cache, and if not, it is retrieved from the source and stored in the cache using the `Set` method.

1.3 Implementing Output Caching

Output caching allows you to cache the output of an entire action or view, reducing the need to re-render the content for subsequent requests. This can significantly improve the performance of frequently accessed pages or views.

To implement output caching, follow these steps:

1. Apply the `[OutputCache]` attribute to the action or view that you want to cache.

```csharp
[OutputCache(Duration = 3600)] // Cache the output for 1 hour
public ActionResult Index()
{
    // Action code
    return View();
}
```

```
[OutputCache(Duration = 3600)] // Cache the output for 1 hour
public ActionResult Index()
{
    // Action code
    return View();
}
```

In this example, the `[OutputCache]` attribute is applied to the `Index` action, specifying a cache duration of 1 hour. This means that the output of the action will be cached for 1 hour, and subsequent requests will be served from the cache without re-executing the action code or rendering the view.

1.4 Implementing Client-side Caching

Client-side caching allows the client to cache resources, such as scripts, stylesheets, or images, reducing the need to re-download them for subsequent requests. This can improve the overall performance and reduce network traffic.

To implement client-side caching, you can utilize HTTP headers, such as the `Cache-Control` and `Expires` headers, to instruct the client's browser to cache the resources.

```csharp
public ActionResult SomeAction()
{
    // Action code

    // Set cache-related HTTP headers
    Response.Cache.SetCacheability(HttpCacheability.Public);

    Response.Cache.SetExpires(DateTime.Now.AddMinutes(30)); // Cache for 30 minutes

    return View();
```

}

```
```

```
public ActionResult SomeAction()
{
    // Action code

    // Set cache-related HTTP headers
    Response.Cache.SetCacheability(HttpCacheability.Public);
    Response.Cache.SetExpires(DateTime.Now.AddMinutes(30)); // Cache for 30 minutes

    return View();
}
```

In this example, the `SetCacheability` method is used to specify that the response can be cached by the client. The `SetExpires` method sets the expiration time for the cached content.

1.5 Summary

Implementing caching in ASP.NET MVC can significantly improve performance by reducing the need for repetitive computations, database queries, and rendering of content. By utilizing server-side caching, output caching, and client-side caching techniques, you can optimize the performance of your application and enhance the overall user experience.

Exercises:

1. Identify areas in your ASP.NET MVC application where caching can be implemented for performance optimization.

2. Implement server-side caching for frequently accessed data or computations.

3. Apply output caching to specific actions or views to improve response times.

4. Configure client-side caching for static resources to reduce network traffic.

Chapter 2: Working with Web API and JSON Serialization

In this chapter, we will explore working with Web API and JSON serialization in ASP.NET MVC. Web API allows you to build HTTP-based services that can be consumed by various clients, and JSON serialization is a common way to represent data in Web API responses.

2.1 Introducing Web API

Web API is a framework in ASP.NET MVC that allows you to build HTTP-based services, commonly known as APIs (Application Programming Interfaces). Web API enables you to expose your application's data and functionality to other systems or clients, such as mobile applications or third-party integrations.

With Web API, you can easily build RESTful services by defining routes, handling HTTP verbs, and returning data in various formats, such as JSON or XML. JSON (JavaScript Object Notation) has become a popular format for data representation in Web API due to its simplicity and ease of use.

2.2 Creating Web API Controllers

To create a Web API controller in ASP.NET MVC, follow these steps:

1. Add a new controller to your ASP.NET MVC project.

2. Inherit the controller from the `ApiController` class instead of the `Controller` class.

```csharp
public class MyApiController : ApiController
{
    // Web API actions and methods
}
```

```
public class MyApiController : ApiController
{
    // Web API actions and methods
}
```

3. Define actions within the controller to handle HTTP requests.

```csharp
public class MyApiController : ApiController
{
    [HttpGet]
```

```csharp
public IHttpActionResult GetData()

{

    // Retrieve and return data

    return Ok(data);

}


[HttpPost]

public IHttpActionResult AddData(DataModel data)

{

    // Process and add data

    return CreatedAtRoute("DefaultApi", new { id = data.Id }, data);

}

}
```
```
```

```
public class MyApiController : ApiController
{
    [HttpGet]
    public IHttpActionResult GetData()
    {
        // Retrieve and return data
        return Ok(data);
    }

    [HttpPost]
    public IHttpActionResult AddData(DataModel data)
    {
        // Process and add data
        return CreatedAtRoute("DefaultApi", new { id = data.Id }, data);
    }
}
```

In this example, the `GetData` action handles the HTTP GET request
and returns data using the `Ok` method, while the `AddData` action
handles the HTTP POST request and adds data, returning the newly
created data and a location header using the `CreatedAtRoute`
method.

2.3 JSON Serialization in Web API

JSON serialization is the process of converting .NET objects into JSON
format for transmission over the network. In Web API, JSON
serialization is handled by default, allowing you to return .NET
objects from Web API actions, and they will be automatically
serialized into JSON.

To return JSON data from a Web API action, follow these steps:

1. Define the return type of the action as `IHttpActionResult` or `HttpResponseMessage`.

2. Return the data as an object or a strongly-typed model.

```csharp
public IHttpActionResult GetData()
{
    var data = GetSomeData();
    return Ok(data);
}
```

```
public IHttpActionResult GetData()
{
    var data = GetSomeData();
    return Ok(data);
}
```

In this example, the `GetData` action returns the `data` object using the `Ok` method, which serializes the data into JSON format.

2.4 Configuring JSON Serialization

You can configure various aspects of JSON serialization in Web API, such as controlling the formatting, handling circular references, or customizing serialization settings. This can be done using the

`JsonSerializerSettings` class or by modifying the `JsonFormatter` in the Web API configuration.

To configure JSON serialization, follow these steps:

1. Modify the `JsonFormatter` settings in the Web API configuration.

```csharp
config.Formatters.JsonFormatter.SerializerSettings.Formatting = Formatting.Indented;

config.Formatters.JsonFormatter.SerializerSettings.ReferenceLoopHandling = ReferenceLoopHandling.Ignore;
```

```
config.Formatters.JsonFormatter.SerializerSettings.Formatting = Formatting.Indented;
config.Formatters.JsonFormatter.SerializerSettings.ReferenceLoopHandling = ReferenceLoopHandling.Ignore
;
```

In this example, the `Formatting` property is set to `Formatting.Indented`, which adds indentation to the serialized JSON output. The `ReferenceLoopHandling` property is set to `ReferenceLoopHandling.Ignore`, which handles circular references by ignoring them during serialization.

2.5 Summary

Working with Web API and JSON serialization in ASP.NET MVC allows you to build HTTP-based services and transmit data in JSON format.

By creating Web API controllers, defining actions to handle HTTP requests, and leveraging JSON serialization, you can expose your application's functionality and data to other systems or clients in a RESTful manner.

Exercises:

1. Create a Web API controller in your ASP.NET MVC application.

2. Define actions within the controller to handle HTTP requests and return data in JSON format.

3. Test the Web API endpoints using a tool like Postman or by integrating them with a client application.

Chapter 3: Integrating Client-Side Technologies (JavaScript, jQuery)

In this chapter, we will explore integrating client-side technologies, such as JavaScript and jQuery, into your ASP.NET MVC application. Integrating client-side technologies allows you to enhance the user experience and add dynamic functionality to your application.

3.1 Working with JavaScript in ASP.NET MVC

JavaScript is a widely used scripting language that runs on the client-side. It enables you to add interactivity and dynamic behavior to your web pages. In ASP.NET MVC, you can easily work with JavaScript by including it in your views or separate JavaScript files.

To work with JavaScript in ASP.NET MVC, follow these steps:

1. Include JavaScript code directly in your views using `<script>` tags.

```html
<script>
  // JavaScript code
  function myFunction() {
    // Function logic
```

```
    }
</script>
```

```
<script>
    // JavaScript code
    function myFunction() {
        // Function logic
    }
</script>
```

2. Organize your JavaScript code in separate files and include them in your views.

```html
<script src="~/Scripts/myScript.js"></script>
```

```
<script src="~/Scripts/myScript.js"></script>
```

3. Access ASP.NET MVC model data in JavaScript by rendering it in your views.

```html
<script>
    var data = @Html.Raw(Json.Encode(Model));
```

</script>

```
```

```
<script>
    var data = @Html.Raw(Json.Encode(Model));
</script>
```

In this example, the `@Html.Raw(Json.Encode(Model))` expression is used to encode the ASP.NET MVC model data into JSON format and include it as a JavaScript variable.

3.2 Using jQuery in ASP.NET MVC

jQuery is a popular JavaScript library that simplifies HTML document traversal, event handling, and AJAX interactions. It provides a wide range of utility functions and makes it easier to manipulate the HTML DOM and interact with the server.

To use jQuery in ASP.NET MVC, follow these steps:

1. Include the jQuery library in your project by downloading it or using a CDN.

```html
<script src="https://code.jquery.com/jquery-3.6.0.min.js"></script>
```

```
<script src="https://code.jquery.com/jquery-3.6.0.min.js"></script>
```

2. Use jQuery functions to interact with HTML elements and handle events.

```html
<script>
    $(document).ready(function() {
        // jQuery code
        $('#myButton').click(function() {
            // Handle button click event
        });
    });
</script>
```

```
<script>
    $(document).ready(function() {
        // jQuery code
        $('#myButton').click(function() {
            // Handle button click event
        });
    });
</script>
```

In this example, the `$(document).ready` function is used to ensure that the jQuery code executes when the document is ready. The `click` function is used to handle the click event of an HTML element with the `myButton` ID.

3. Make AJAX requests to the server using jQuery's AJAX functions.

```javascript
$.ajax({
    url: '/Controller/Action',
    type: 'GET',
    data: { parameter1: value1, parameter2: value2 },
    success: function(response) {
        // Handle the server response
    },
    error: function(error) {
        // Handle errors
    }
});
```

```
$.ajax({
    url: '/Controller/Action',
    type: 'GET',
    data: { parameter1: value1, parameter2: value2 },
    success: function(response) {
        // Handle the server response
    },
    error: function(error) {
        // Handle errors
    }
});
```

In this example, the `$.ajax` function is used to make a GET request to a specific controller action, passing parameters and handling the success and error responses.

3.3 Summary

Integrating client-side technologies, such as JavaScript and jQuery, into your ASP.NET MVC application allows you to add interactivity, manipulate the HTML DOM, and perform AJAX interactions with the server. By working with JavaScript in your views, using jQuery to simplify client-side coding, and making AJAX requests to the server, you can enhance the user experience and add dynamic functionality to your application.

Exercises:

1. Add JavaScript code to your ASP.NET MVC views to enhance interactivity.

2. Use jQuery functions to handle events and manipulate the HTML DOM.

3. Make AJAX requests to the server using jQuery's AJAX functions.

Chapter 4: Unit Testing and Test-Driven Development (TDD)

In this chapter, we will explore unit testing and test-driven development (TDD) in the context of ASP.NET MVC. Unit testing allows you to verify the behavior of individual components or units of your application, ensuring that they function correctly. TDD is an approach where tests are written before the actual code, helping to drive the development process.

4.1 Understanding Unit Testing

Unit testing is the practice of testing individual units or components of your application in isolation. In ASP.NET MVC, units can include controllers, models, services, or any other discrete units of functionality. The goal of unit testing is to ensure that each unit works as expected and produces the correct results.

Unit testing typically involves the following steps:

1. Write a test: Create a test method that exercises a specific behavior or functionality of a unit.

2. Set up test data: Prepare the necessary data or dependencies for the unit being tested.

3. Invoke the unit: Call the method or operation being tested with the provided test data.

4. Assert the result: Verify that the actual result matches the expected outcome using assertions.

By writing comprehensive unit tests, you can detect and fix issues early in the development process, promote code quality, and facilitate future changes or refactoring.

4.2 Test-Driven Development (TDD)

Test-Driven Development (TDD) is a development approach that emphasizes writing tests before writing the actual code. With TDD, you follow a cyclical process of "Red-Green-Refactor":

1. Red: Write a failing test that describes the desired behavior of the unit being developed. This step ensures that you have a clear understanding of the expected functionality.

2. Green: Write the minimum amount of code required to make the failing test pass. This step focuses on implementing the necessary functionality to meet the test criteria.

3. Refactor: Improve the code structure, remove duplication, and enhance overall design without changing the observed behavior. This step ensures that the codebase remains clean and maintainable.

By following the TDD cycle, you iteratively build your application, continuously running tests to verify that the existing codebase remains functional and regression-free.

4.3 Unit Testing in ASP.NET MVC

ASP.NET MVC provides a robust framework for unit testing. You can use testing frameworks like NUnit, xUnit, or MSTest to write and execute unit tests for your controllers, models, and other components.

To create unit tests in ASP.NET MVC, follow these steps:

1. Set up the testing environment: Install the necessary testing framework and any additional testing libraries you may require.

2. Write tests for controllers: Test the behavior of your controllers by simulating HTTP requests and asserting the expected responses.

3. Write tests for models and services: Test the logic and functionality of your models and services, ensuring that they produce the correct results.

4. Run tests and analyze results: Execute the unit tests and review the test results to identify any failures or issues.

By regularly running unit tests as part of your development process, you can quickly detect and resolve any problems, improving the quality and reliability of your ASP.NET MVC application.

4.4 Summary

Unit testing and test-driven development (TDD) are essential practices in ASP.NET MVC development. By writing comprehensive unit tests and following the TDD cycle of "Red-Green-Refactor," you can ensure the correctness of your code, detect issues early, and maintain a high level of code quality. ASP.NET MVC provides a solid foundation for unit testing, allowing you to test controllers, models, services, and other components of your application.

Exercises:

1. Set up a testing framework, such as NUnit or xUnit, in your ASP.NET MVC project.

2. Write unit tests for your controllers, models, or services, covering different scenarios and edge cases.

3. Practice the TDD approach by writing failing tests, implementing the required functionality, and refactoring the code.

Chapter 5: Deployment and Hosting Options

In this final chapter, we will explore deployment and hosting options for ASP.NET MVC applications. Deploying your application to a production environment and choosing the right hosting option are critical steps in making your application accessible to users.

5.1 Deployment Strategies

When it comes to deploying an ASP.NET MVC application, there are various strategies you can follow. Some common deployment strategies include:

1. File System Deployment: Copying the application files to a target server's file system manually.

2. Web Deploy: Using Microsoft Web Deploy tool to publish the application directly to a web server or hosting provider.

3. FTP Deployment: Uploading the application files to the server using FTP (File Transfer Protocol).

4. Continuous Integration/Continuous Deployment (CI/CD): Automating the deployment process by integrating with CI/CD tools like Azure DevOps, Jenkins, or GitHub Actions.

The deployment strategy you choose depends on factors such as your hosting environment, team requirements, and deployment automation needs.

5.2 Hosting Options

ASP.NET MVC applications can be hosted on various platforms and hosting providers. Here are some common hosting options:

1. Self-Hosting: Hosting the application on your own infrastructure or server. This gives you full control but requires managing the server, including security, updates, and maintenance.

2. Shared Hosting: Using shared hosting services where multiple applications share the same server and resources. Shared hosting is cost-effective but may have limitations on performance and scalability.

3. Virtual Private Server (VPS) Hosting: Renting a virtual server that provides dedicated resources for your application. VPS hosting offers more control and scalability than shared hosting.

4. Cloud Hosting: Deploying the application on cloud platforms like Microsoft Azure, Amazon Web Services (AWS), or Google Cloud

Platform (GCP). Cloud hosting offers scalability, flexibility, and managed services, but it may involve additional costs.

5. Platform as a Service (PaaS): Using a PaaS provider like Azure App Service or Heroku to host and manage your application. PaaS providers handle infrastructure management, scaling, and other operational tasks.

Choose a hosting option based on your application's requirements, scalability needs, budget, and the level of control and management you desire.

5.3 Security Considerations

When deploying an ASP.NET MVC application, it's crucial to address security considerations. Some key security practices include:

1. Secure Connections: Use HTTPS (HTTP over SSL/TLS) to ensure secure communication between the client and server, especially for sensitive data.

2. Authentication and Authorization: Implement proper authentication and authorization mechanisms to control access to your application and protect sensitive resources.

3. Secure Configuration: Ensure that sensitive configuration settings, such as database connection strings or API keys, are properly secured and not exposed in the application's source code or configuration files.

4. Regular Updates and Patches: Keep your application and its dependencies up to date with the latest security patches and updates.

5. Web Application Firewall (WAF): Consider using a WAF to add an extra layer of protection against common web application security threats.

Ensure you follow security best practices and perform regular security audits to mitigate potential vulnerabilities in your application.

5.4 Summary

Deploying and hosting an ASP.NET MVC application involves choosing a deployment strategy, selecting the right hosting option, and addressing security considerations. By selecting an appropriate deployment strategy, such as file system deployment or using CI/CD tools, and choosing the right hosting option, such as self-hosting, shared hosting, VPS hosting, cloud hosting, or PaaS, you can make your application accessible to users. Additionally, addressing security considerations is essential to protect your application and its data.

Exercises:

1. Choose a deployment strategy that suits your project requirements and deploy your ASP.NET MVC application to a production environment.

2. Explore different hosting options and select the one that best fits your application's needs.

3. Implement necessary security measures, such as HTTPS, authentication, and secure configuration, in your deployed application.

Conclusion: Journey Towards ASP.NET MVC Mastery

Congratulations on completing your journey towards ASP.NET MVC mastery! Throughout this learning experience, you have gained a solid understanding of ASP.NET MVC and acquired valuable skills to develop robust web applications. Let's take a moment to reflect on your accomplishments and outline the key takeaways from your journey.

1. Getting Started: You began by understanding the basics of ASP.NET MVC, including its architecture, key components, and advantages over other web frameworks. You set up the development environment and explored the project structure, laying the foundation for your ASP.NET MVC applications.

2. Building the Model: You delved into the model in ASP.NET MVC, learning how to create model classes, implement data access with Entity Framework, and use data annotations for validation. You also tested your model classes to ensure their functionality.

3. Developing the Views: You focused on creating views in ASP.NET MVC, including view templates using Razor syntax, working with

layouts and partial views, implementing forms and HTML helpers, and styling and customizing views. You learned how to create visually appealing and interactive user interfaces.

4. Controllers and Routing: You gained a deep understanding of controllers and routing in ASP.NET MVC. You learned to implement controller actions, handle parameters and model binding, and configure routing rules for mapping URLs to controllers and actions. You also explored error handling and exception management.

5. Working with Data and Entity Framework: You learned how to retrieve, display, sort, filter, update, and delete data in ASP.NET MVC using Entity Framework. You explored advanced querying techniques to perform complex data operations efficiently.

6. Authentication and Authorization: You explored authentication and authorization in ASP.NET MVC, including implementing user registration and login, securing controllers and actions, and implementing role-based authorization. You also customized authentication and authorization to meet specific application requirements.

7. Advanced Topics and Best Practices: You delved into advanced topics such as implementing caching for performance optimization, working with Web API and JSON serialization, integrating client-side technologies like JavaScript and jQuery, and unit testing and test-driven development (TDD) to ensure code quality.

8. Deployment and Hosting Options: Finally, you learned about different deployment strategies, hosting options, and security considerations when deploying and hosting ASP.NET MVC applications.

By completing these chapters and exercises, you have developed a strong foundation in ASP.NET MVC and acquired the skills necessary to build robust and scalable web applications. Remember to continue practicing and exploring new features, as ASP.NET MVC is a dynamic framework that constantly evolves.

Keep in mind these key takeaways from your journey:

1. MVC Architecture: Understand the Model-View-Controller architecture and how it separates concerns in your application.

2. Development Environment: Set up your development environment and familiarize yourself with the project structure to efficiently build ASP.NET MVC applications.

3. Models, Views, and Controllers: Understand how to create models, develop views using Razor syntax, and implement controllers to handle user requests and logic.

4. Entity Framework: Utilize Entity Framework for data access, database operations, and implementing advanced querying techniques.

5. Authentication and Authorization: Implement secure authentication and authorization mechanisms to protect your application's resources.

6. Client-Side Technologies: Integrate JavaScript, jQuery, and other client-side technologies to enhance the user experience and add interactivity.

7. Testing and Quality Assurance: Embrace unit testing and test-driven development (TDD) to ensure code quality, reliability, and maintainability.

8. Deployment and Hosting: Choose the appropriate deployment strategy, select the right hosting option, and address security considerations when deploying your ASP.NET MVC application.

Remember, mastering ASP.NET MVC is an ongoing journey. Stay up-to-date with the latest advancements, explore additional features and libraries, and leverage best practices to continuously improve your skills.

Congratulations once again on your achievement! Embrace the knowledge and experience gained throughout this journey, and apply it to real-world projects. Happy coding with ASP.NET MVC!

www.ingramcontent.com/pod-product-compliance
Lightning Source LLC
LaVergne TN
LVHW051320050326
832903LV00031B/3282